AF593901

Footpath Touring

with Ken Ward

Land's End and The Lizard

My mind lets go of many things,
Like mists and mud and chilly winds.
And yet recalls the bluebell slopes, and orchards rare,
The tiny Thrift, low and fast against the gale,
The thundering waves upon the shore,
The churchyard stone, '120 men lie here,'
The seagull white against the storm,
then black against the snowy cloud.

A treasured time to listen, see and think
And then the final strange sad joy of a journey's end.

Catherine Seeley
Ithaca, USA

You can only see Cornwall or know anything about it by walking through it.

George Borrow
Novelist and Traveller
1803–1881

Jarrold Colour Publications, Norwich

All about Footpath-Touring

This spectacular Footpath-Touring adventure will take you along the most magnificent section of the 563 mile *904 km* South West Peninsula Coastal Path

The route: The route has been divided into daily stages well within the capabilities of those quite new to walking. More experienced walkers, are, of course, free to extend these stages as they wish.

Getting there: Full details of public transport and car-parking facilities are given on page 6.

Accommodation: Green information panels included on the maps contain advice on overnight accommodation. Unless mentioned, all will provide an evening meal. All have become known to me during my time of walking and research for this guide. I offer them in good faith, without accepting responsibility for them.

Those places where I received a particularly warm welcome are surrounded by a box.

The accommodation is divided into three price categories; economy, medium, and not-cheap. All provide reasonable value while some can be outstandingly good. I suggest you always check costs when making reservations, and remember to check that VAT is included.

Where possible the exact locations of accommodation are indicated, however telephone numbers are given should directions be required.

Out of season it should be sufficient to make telephone reservations the day before. This gives you great flexibility in your programme allowing you to take non-walking days to suit inclinations and weather. In high holiday seasons reservations should be made as early as possible. (For non-walking days see page 4.) We recommend that you make it quite clear if an evening meal is required, and, if possible, give some indication of time of arrival.

Please mention Footpath-Touring when booking as all accommodations have been asked to suggest an alternative should they be fully booked.

All accommodations have been selected for their appreciation of the needs of Footpath-Touring walkers particularly regarding warm rooms, good food, drying facilities, early starts, and packed lunches.

Where the accommodation is a pub or a licensed establishment this is indicated.

Two letters after the name show the period that accommodation is available, for example, A/O=April to October, M/N=March to November. Those open all year are identified with an □, however remember that during winter months they may be decorating, taking holidays, or repairing burst water-pipes!

What you will need: Remember that you will be carrying your baggage on your back so keep it light!

You will need clothes to walk in, boots, waterproofs, clothes for the evenings, night-wear, toiletries, and little more. These are dealt with below.

Clothes to walk in: There is no need ever to be uncomfortable when walking. If you are sweating or are cold you are doing something wrong. Consider your clothing as a layer insulating system that is capable of being added to or decreased as conditions demand. Great flexibility is possible by using layers of thin garments rather than a few thick items. Wherever possible make use of shirts and woollens that button down the front. These are easy to put on and take off, and give a subtle degree of control by using the buttons. Natural fibres like wool and cotton are to be preferred.

Outdoors shops stock special walking trousers or breeches but good-quality trousers purchased anywhere can be equally useful. Jeans are useless. Despite their outdoor image they trap no heat and once wet take a long time to dry. Ladies will probably find trousers more practical than skirts.

With our uncertain climate, gloves can be just as useful in flaming June as in December. Remember, too, that the head is responsible for a very large heat loss and a woollen hat or Balaclava helmet can provide a great deal of comfort.

A windproof jacket of tight-weave material is essential. This should be front opening, with plenty of pockets, and preferably have a hood.

Boots: I consider it essential to wear boots when Footpath-Touring along this coast. Many of the paths are very stony and steep. Boots will give the necessary support to your ankles and cushion the soles of your feet. Heed the advice of your local reputable outdoors shop, and select comfortable, lightweight walking-boots. And wear them as much as possible before you begin Footpath-Touring. These boots are your wheels and you carry no spare. Choose wisely.

Waterproofs: Assume that during your tour there will be wet days. Rain is no hardship if you are properly protected.

You will need a lightweight waterproof jacket with hood, pockets, and front opening. Lightweight waterproof over-trousers that can be slipped over booted feet are also essential. You are strongly advised to equip yourself with lightweight gaiters that go from boot to knee, and I recommend you wear them on all but the driest days. Even when there is no rain they will prevent trouser bottoms from getting wet and heavy from long, dew-laden grass or cliff-path mud. And when you arrive at that hostelry, a flick of the wrist and you could be straight from Savile Row!

Clothes for the evening: This is where your ingenuity comes into its own. It is necessary for you to devise a wardrobe that will meet any requirements but will weigh practically nothing. The following check-list may be useful and give you some ideas.

Ladies: Pullover
Blouse
Lightweight crease-resistant trousers or skirt
Lightweight crease-resistant jacket
Coloured scarves to provide some variety
Underclothes
Light shoes
Night-wear
Handkerchiefs
Toiletries

Remember that you will be staying at a different address every night and any variety is to please only yourself or your Footpath-Touring companions!

Men: Shirt
Pullover
Lightweight crease-resistant trousers
Lightweight crease-resistant jacket (a safari suit is ideal)
Tie
Underclothes
Socks
Night-wear
Handkerchiefs
Toiletries

But do keep it light!

It is possible to buy lightweight haversacks which pack to the size of a lady's purse. These are ideal for packing evening-wear inside your main pack. And they also provide a useful carrier should you wish to walk anytime without your main pack. (See Non-baggage-carrying days; page 4.)

Toiletries: Your normal toiletries and make-up kit should not weigh more than 9 ounces! This can easily be achieved by searching for the smallest packs and refusing to carry glass.

Men who normally use an electric razor might consider using disposable razors for the tour, but remember to take the smallest tube of brushless cream, and a styptic pencil.

Rucksack: Assemble all the items you plan to take with you and weigh them.

Ideally this total weight should not exceed 11 lb for an adult man. It is absolutely essential that on no account should it weigh more than 12 lb. Ladies should aim for about 2 lb less depending upon build. Keep trimming until this weight limit is achieved.

You will find that you will need a rucksack with a capacity of about 35 litres. Most shops offer a choice of a rucksack with an outside light metal frame, an internal frame, or no frame at all. I strongly recommend the metal frame variety. A padded hip-belt is essential. This, when fitted across the hips (not round the waist), ensures that the load is carried on the pelvis and not from the shoulders. Shoulder-straps should be wide and padded. When buying I suggest you ask the salesman to load the pack and allow you to walk round his shop. It is essential that the pack feels comfortable.

Water-bottle: It is sensible to have a small water-bottle with you.

Lunches: Most Footpath-Touring routes are arranged so that about midday the walker is near an establishment where refreshments can be obtained. However, this coastal walk requires packed lunches on some days. These days are indicated in the guide. A small vacuum flask would be a useful item to carry for these lunch-breaks.

Non-walking days: You may walk the whole route in consecutive days. However, if you are new to walking you are urged to include some non-walking days. These will enable you to take a late breakfast, explore the area, or merely lick wounds. (See page 5.)

If poor weather or other causes suggest taking an unscheduled non-walking day, the next overnight stop can always be joined by taxi.

Any of the taxi-operators detailed on the maps will transport you. Always ask the fare first, and mention Footpath-Touring to get the benefit of any advantageous rates.

Non-baggage-carrying days: If the luxury of a non-baggage-carrying day appeals to you then the same taxi-operators will transport your pack during the morning. Again check charges first and mention Footpath-Touring to benefit from reasonable rates. This is where your lightweight haversack, suggested on page 3, will be indispensable for carrying wet gear, camera, and snacks.

Guardian Angels: On some of the maps you will see details of Guardian Angels spread along the route. Should a situation develop during a day when a telephone call becomes essential you may call on these kindly Angels for help. They are all volunteers, of course, and any calls made should be paid for.

Good behaviour: Many people walk this coast path. Most behave in a responsible and thoughtful manner. Unfortunately a few do not. Please be most careful about reclosing gates, keeping dogs under control, causing no damage, and leaving no litter. Please.

Maps: The guide maps together with the directions, allow you to easily follow the route. However, I suggest that you may wish to equip yourself with the excellent Ordnance Survey 1:50 000 maps which will enable you to identify features inland and distant headlands.

Sheet 203, Land's End and Lizard covers the whole of the route from Pendeen to Lizard. Sheet 204, Truro and Falmouth, is required for the Lizard to Coverack extension.

About this Land's End and Lizard tour

You can complete this Footpath-Touring route in a week of steady walking, including a half-day off mid-week, so that your programme might look like this:

Friday	Travel to Penzance and Pendeen (see page 6)
Saturday	Walk to Sennen Cove
Sunday	Walk via Land's End to Porthcurno
Monday	Walk to Mousehole
Tuesday	Bus to Penzance (or walk by road); Explore, shop, and rest. Boat excursion to beautiful St Michael's Mount.
Wednesday	Early morning bus to Marazion. Walk to Prah Sands
Thursday	Walk to Mullion Cove
Friday	Walk to Lizard
Saturday	Travel home (see page 7)

However, this is a wonderful part of Britain with a great deal to see, and you are urged to spread the tour over as many days as possible. Your tour might even look like this:

First day	Travel to Penzance and Pendeen (see page 6)
Second day	Explore Pendeen (see below). Prepare for walk
Third day	Walk to Sennen Cove
Fourth day	Walk via Land's End to Porthcurno
Fifth day	Walk to Mousehole
Sixth day	Morning in Mousehole. Afternoon bus to Penzance (or walk by road)
Seventh day	Day in Penzance to rest, explore, and shop (see page 29) Boat excursion to St Michael's Mount (see opening days page 29) Or take a day trip to the Isles of Scilly, by steamboat or by helicopter (see page 29) Or take a flight over the coast path in a three-seater aircraft (see page 29)
Eighth day	Morning bus to Marazion. Walk to Prah Sands
Ninth day	Walk to Mullion Cove
Tenth day	Walk to Lizard
Eleventh day	Walk extension to Coverack
Twelfth day	Travel home (see page 7)

A wonderful tour!

When to go

During the summer, blue skies and blue-green seas can often justify the description 'the Cornish Riviera'. Long days can mean lazy schedules with time for cliff-top dozing under warm sea breezes.

But the spring and autumn have their own special attractions. Beaches are empty, and the little harbours and villages are for you alone. Spring flowers carpet the cliff tops in a blaze of colour; while the autumn offers changing leaves, bracken, heather, and dramatic, pounding seas.

In short, any time of the year provides excellent walking with marvellous sea and coastal scenery.

Exploring Pendeen

If you are in Pendeen on the day before your walk, with time to spare, you can stretch your legs with the splendid circular route shown on pages 8 and 9. Begin with a visit to the Geevor Mine Museum (perhaps also the ore-treatment plant, which takes about an hour), from there take the Footpath-Tour route down to Pendeen Watch and visit the lighthouse. From there follow the Footpath-Touring route through the ruins of Levant Mine to Carn Du. Turn Left up Levant Lane to Trewellard and Pendeen. Next morning, return down Levant Lane to rejoin the Footpath-Touring route at Carn Du.

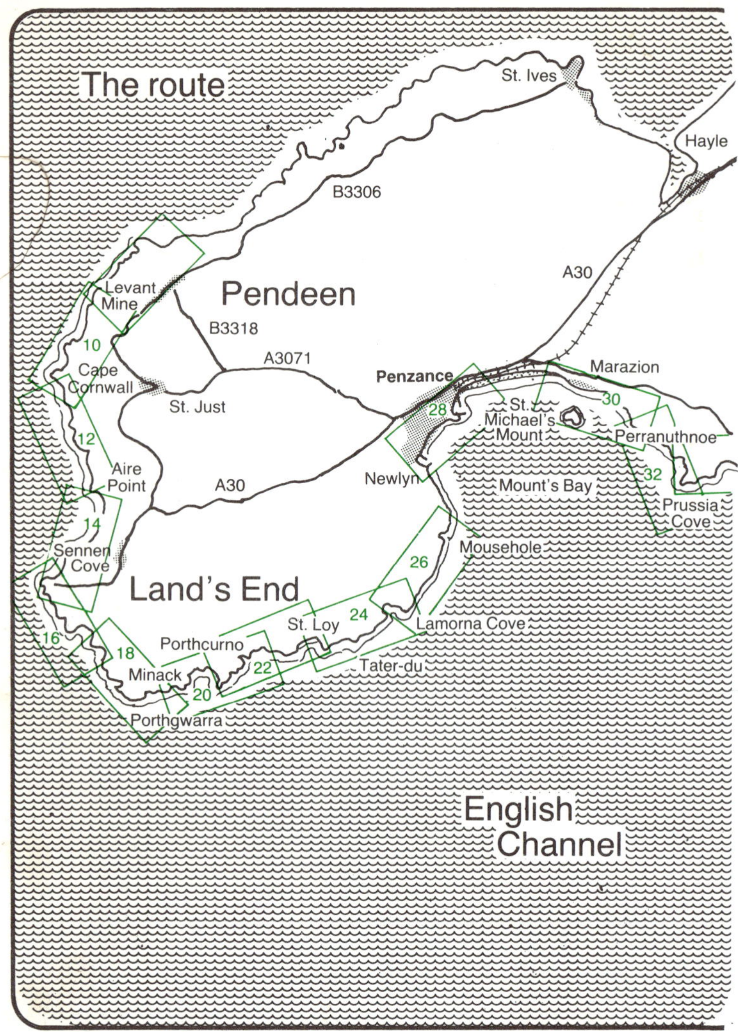

Getting to Pendeen

By rail: British Rail operates trains to Penzance from Paddington, London and Birmingham every day of the year. A night sleeper service runs from Paddington, London every evening.

From Penzance to Pendeen: Western National operate regular buses, Monday to Saturday, Service 17. Bus station opposite railway station. Enquiries telephone 0736 62274.

Carne's Taxis, all year, telephone 0736 63572.

By coach: National Express operate coach services throughout the year to Penzance.

By car: Cars can be parked at Pendeen Filling Station for about £5 per week. Enquiries telephone 0736 788387. However, we recommend you park your car in Penzance, and take the bus to Pendeen, (see above). This makes returning to car at end of Footpath-Touring less complicated (see opposite).
Avalon Garage, Regent Terrace, Penzance (see page 28). About £14 per week under cover. Enquiries telephone 0736 64622

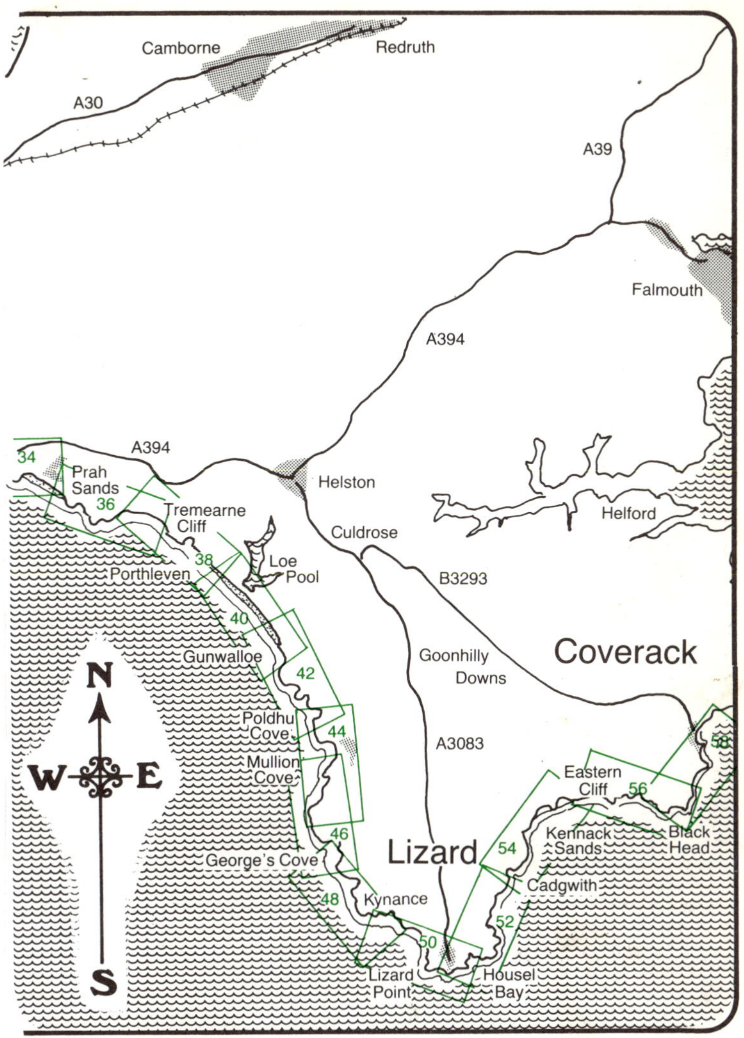

Travel from Lizard: Buses leave from Lizard for Helston at 09.00 hrs and 14.09 hrs Monday to Saturday, all year.
Buses, Helston to Penzance, leave every hour, on the hour, 07.00 hrs to 18.00 hrs, Monday to Saturday, all year.
In summer a Sunday service operates. Enquiries to Western National, telephone 0872 40404.

Telvyn Farm Taxis, all year, telephone 0326 290471

Travel from Coverack: Buses leave Coverack for Helston on Monday, Thursday (10.25 hrs) and Saturday (09.25 hrs).
Enquiries to Trelawney Tours, telephone 0736 850702
For Helston to Penzance see above.

Zoar Garage Taxis, all year, telephone 0326 280325

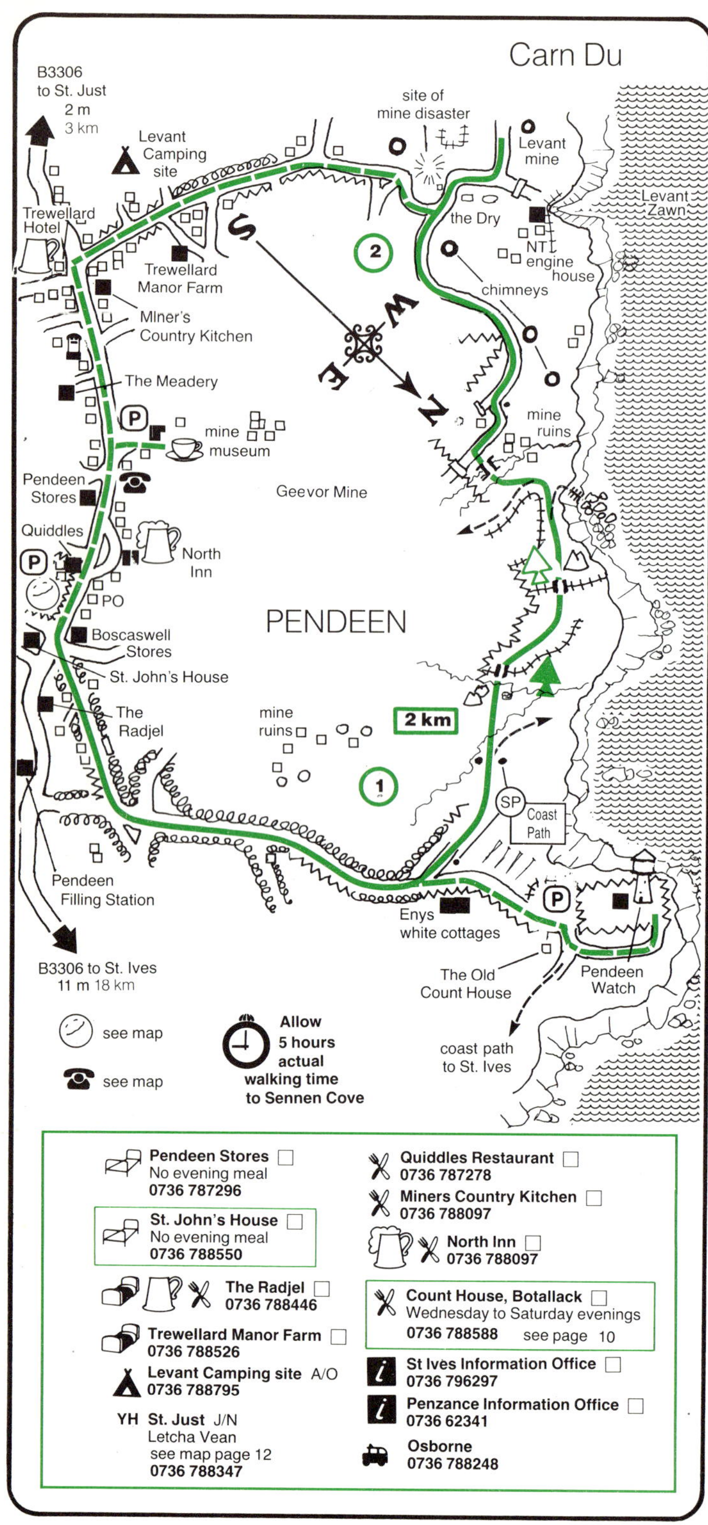
Carn Du
B3306
to St. Just
2 m
3 km
Levant
Camping
site
site of
mine disaster
Levant
mine
Levant
Zawn
Trewellard
Hotel
the Dry
NT
engine
house
Trewellard
Manor Farm
chimneys
Miner's
Country Kitchen
S
W
E
N
The Meadery
P
mine
museum
mine
ruins
Pendeen
Stores
Geevor Mine
Quiddles
P
North
Inn
PO
PENDEEN
Boscaswell
Stores
St. John's House
The
Radjel
mine
ruins
2 km
1
2
SP
Coast
Path
P
Pendeen
Filling Station
Enys
white cottages
The Old
Count House
Pendeen
Watch
B3306 to St. Ives
11 m 18 km
see map
see map
Allow
5 hours
actual
walking time
to Sennen Cove
coast path
to St. Ives
Pendeen Stores
No evening meal
0736 787296
St. John's House
No evening meal
0736 788550
The Radjel
0736 788446
Trewellard Manor Farm
0736 788526
Levant Camping site A/O
0736 788795
YH St. Just J/N
Letcha Vean
see map page 12
0736 788347
Quiddles Restaurant
0736 787278
Miners Country Kitchen
0736 788097
North Inn
0736 788097
Count House, Botallack
Wednesday to Saturday evenings
0736 788588 see page 10
St Ives Information Office
0736 796297
Penzance Information Office
0736 62341
Osborne
0736 788248

Lunch: The Queen Anne Inn in Botallack is about ten minutes from the path. Bar snacks every day.

Pendeen to Carn Du

Going: A good introduction to the coast path, and a melancholy walk through the ruins of a once busy tin-mine workings.

Pendeen is a granite-built village straggling for about a mile *1·5 km* along the Land's End to St Ives coastal road, born out of copper- and tin-mining. Today tin is still mined here but tourism now provides an additional income.

The Geevor Tin Mine is one of only four mines still producing tin in Cornwall, and there have been underground workings here since the 17thC. Present workings reach a depth of over 2000 feet *610 m* and extend for an area of more than 2 square miles *5 sq. km*, part of which now stretches beneath the Atlantic Ocean.

On the site of the old Wethered Shaft the company has established an excellent little museum, which provides a good introduction to Cornwall's mining story.

Tours may also be made round the surface works, where the ore is ground, and then separated on rows of oscillating water-tables. There is an old saying that if you shout down a hole anywhere in the world, a Cornishman will answer. As an example, a Pendeen miner, Richard Oates, went off to Australia where, on 5 February 1869, he and his partner found the largest gold nugget ever mined in the world. This monster was a foot long and a foot wide and was valued then at £9534.

Leave Pendeen down the lane by the Boscaswell Stores, signposted to the lighthouse. Immediately before the row of white cottages on the Right, take the signposted path on the Left. (A diversion can be made to visit the lighthouse three minutes up the road.)

Pendeen Watch Lighthouse came into operation in 1900. Until 1926 it was oil fuelled, but the present 2 000 000 candle power electrical system provides a signal that can be seen up to 20 miles *32 km* away. A visit will enable you to test for yourself the fact that the 2½ ton apparatus, floating on a trough of mercury, can be set in motion by the push of a finger.

Follow the path down to cross the stream, then climb the track up half-Right, to cross the fence at the top. Here is a spectacular view across an area which was once alive with great activity. Descend to mine ruins and follow signposted path which climbs up through old workings.

Note the red discoloration in the sea, due to the discharge from the mine pumps and the ore separation process.

At Levant Road turn Right and Left to follow coast path signs by Levant Mine.

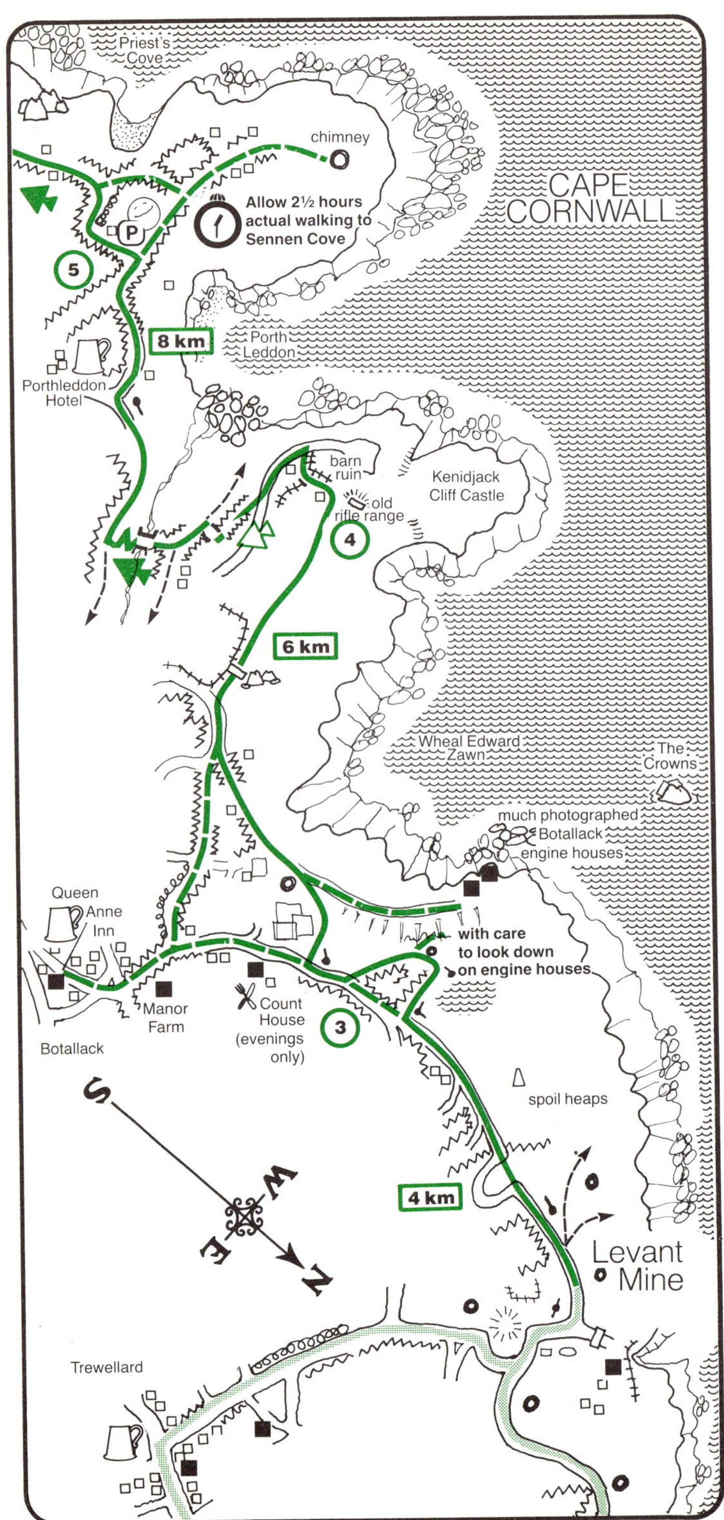
Priest's Cove
chimney
CAPE CORNWALL
Allow 2½ hours actual walking to Sennen Cove
P
5
8 km
Porth Leddon
Porthleddon Hotel
barn ruin
Kenidjack Cliff Castle
old rifle range
4
6 km
Wheal Edward Zawn
The Crowns
much photographed Botallack engine houses
Queen Anne Inn
with care to look down on engine houses
Manor Farm
Count House (evenings only)
3
Botallack
spoil heaps
S
W
E
N
4 km
Levant Mine
Trewellard

Levant Mine to Cape Cornwall

Going: An easy walk through more mine ruins leads to Kenidjack Cliff Castle. From here the path drops down to cross Kenidjack Valley, climbing up the other side to a spectacular, high-level walk to Cape Cornwall.

Levant was one of the great Cornish mines, producing both tin and copper in greater quantities than any other of the Land's End Peninsula mines. Levels at 2000 feet *600 m*, went a mile out to sea. In 1919 there occurred here a terrible disaster (see page 60). The mine finally closed in 1930. A steam whim, or hauling engine, dating from 1840, is preserved in the mine ruins by the National Trust. To visit, apply to Geevor Tin Mines, telephone 0736 788662. A small charge is made.

The wide track leads through mine remains and ancient spoil heaps. After about ten minutes, for some reason, the coast path is signposted round a little loop to the Right, but you may well continue along the track ahead. However, do not miss the thin path that descends through Botallack mine ruins in a few yards on the Right.

For the Queen Anne Inn in Botallack village, continue ahead on the wide track, a ten-minute walk. The Count House restaurant on the Left was once the office building of Botallack Mine. Look for Manor Farm on the Left. The BBC used this as the exterior of Nampara, home of Ross Poldark in the popular television series.. (From Botallack village rejoin Footpath-Touring route by walled lane.)

In the ruins of Botallack Mine, be certain to look back at the engine-houses perched dramatically on the cliffs below. On the grass track leading down to them, the BBC built another 'mine' for Poldark! (See 'Cliff-edge towers of Botallack' on page 61.)

The walled lane from Botallack village rejoins the Footpath-Touring route near the ruin of yet another engine-house. In a few yards, leave the wide track to take the field path off to the Right which leads to the headland and Kenidjack Cliff Castle.

Kenidjack is one of the many Iron Age cliff castles on this stretch of coast. These forts are usually situated on rocky headlands, with one or more protective ramparts inland.

From the barn ruin, drop down to the road and turn Left. Almost immediately take the path Right, which drops down into Kenidjack Valley.

In the valley are the gaunt remains of the Owles Mine. In 1841 this mine employed 200 people and at one time had eight steam-engines working. In 1893 when a flooded section was accidentally holed, the waters rushed into the workings. Twenty-three miners' bodies were never recovered, and the deep levels were abandoned.

Down in the valley, turn Right to cross the valley floor, and climb steeply up the other side. At the top turn Right, and follow the splendid walk round to the road at Cape Cornwall.

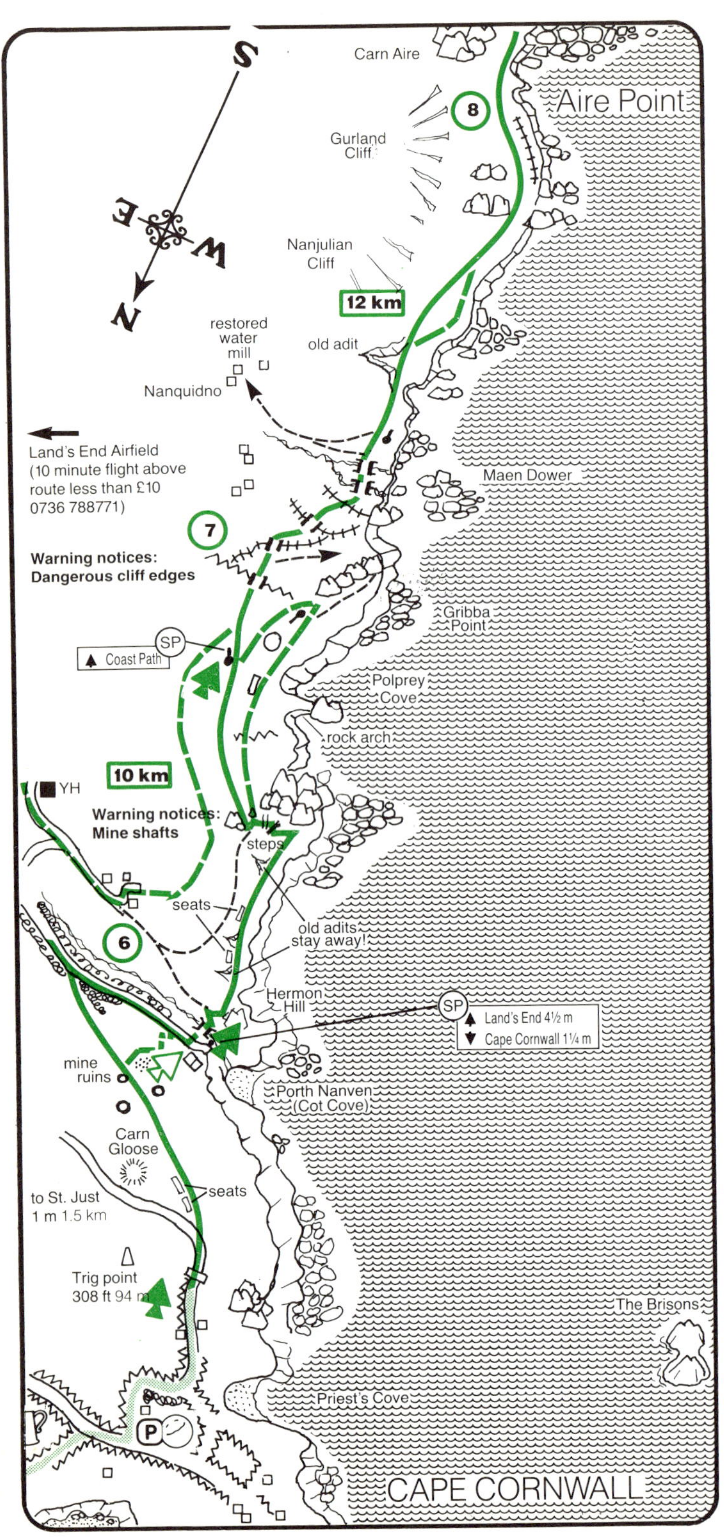
S
E
W
N
Carn Aire
Aire Point
8
Gurland Cliff
Nanjulian Cliff
12 km
restored water mill
old adit
Nanquidno
Land's End Airfield
(10 minute flight above route less than £10 0736 788771)
Maen Dower
7
Warning notices: Dangerous cliff edges
Gribba Point
SP
Coast Path
Polprey Cove
rock arch
10 km
YH
Warning notices: Mine shafts
steps
seats
old adits stay away!
6
Hermon Hill
SP
Land's End 4½ m
Cape Cornwall 1¼ m
mine ruins
Porth Nanven (Cot Cove)
Carn Gloose
seats
to St. Just 1 m 1.5 km
Trig point 308 ft 94 m
The Brisons
Priest's Cove
P
CAPE CORNWALL

Cape Cornwall to Aire Point

Going: Some steep climbs, so adopt a slow steady pace, and enjoy this magnificent coastal walk.

Cape Cornwall, England's only cape, is easily recognised by its hump-shaped headland topped by a tall chimney. In medieval times it was thought to be the most westerly point of England, but Land's End later won that distinction by a few hundred yards. Now the cape stands splendid, and usually deserted.

The chimney was designed to provide a great up-draught, to aid ventilation in the mine 600 feet *180 m* below. It worked much too well and this exotic flue was quickly abandoned.

A walled lane just before the car park climbs steeply up to the headland of Carn Gloose.

A few hundred yards along the road at the top is a large stone barrow which probably dates from 1250 to 1000 BC. Despite learned guesses, its exact purpose is still a mystery.

The path drops gently down through the remains of the St Just United, and the Bosorne and Ballowall United mines. Half-way down, the sure-footed should look for an unsignposted short cut. This thin and rough track drops steeply down by debris, directly to the cove. Mere unhurried mortals should continue down on the main track to the valley road, where turn Right down to Porth Nanven, or Cot Cove.

About a mile *1·6 km* out to sea stand the twin peaks of the cruel Brisons. (See 'A cruel coast' on page 62.)

Cross the small stream, and climb the steps up Hermon Hill.

These steps, and much of the work on the path between here and Maen Dower, are a result of the voluntary labours of Willie Oates, of St Just. Thank you Mr Oates.

An attractive path, just above the sea, leads through the old workings of Wheal Hermon. A few steps lead up by an old shaft, and at the top, if you search around, you will find that Mr Oates has been at work to cut a higher path than the usual route. This avoids a U-turn a bit further on.

The path leads easily up to Gribba Point with its fine views over Whitesand Bay to Sennen Cove and Land's End.

Field stiles lead down into the impressive valley of Nanquidno.

There now follows a most delightful stretch of walking beneath the cliffs of Nanjulian and Gurland. There are various paths, but in general, those only a few feet above the rocky beach are the most interesting.

The rocks of Aire Point make an ideal spot to sit and survey the splendid Whitesand Bay.

Cape View ☐
No evening meal
073 687 671

Myrtle Cottage ☐
073 687 466

Sennen Cove Hotel ☐
073 687 275

Old Success Inn ☐
073 687 232

Trevedra Farm
½ mile 1 km
above Trevedra Cliff
073 687 379

YH St. Just J/N
Letcha Vean
see map page 12
0736 788347

Osborne
0736 788248

see map

see map

Penzance Information Office
0736 62341

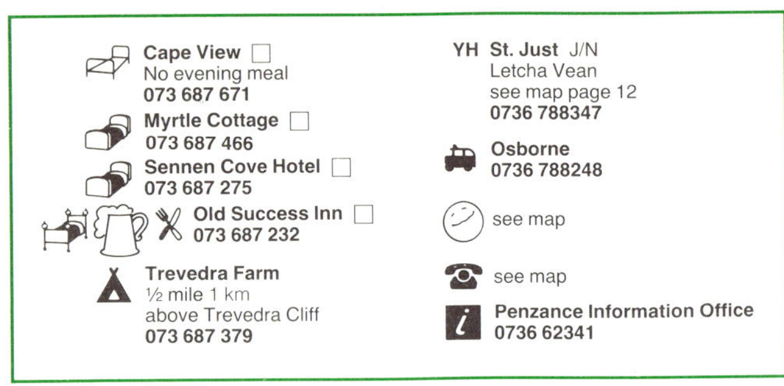

SENNEN COVE
Sennen Cove Hotel
Myrtle Cottage
Old Success
Cape View
bus stop
up to Sennen Village
1m 1.5 km
P
P
stabilising fences
to Sunny Corner
life-boat station
S
W
E
N
9
Whitesand Bay
emergency telephone
14 km
Trevedra Cliff
Gwynver
Aire Point

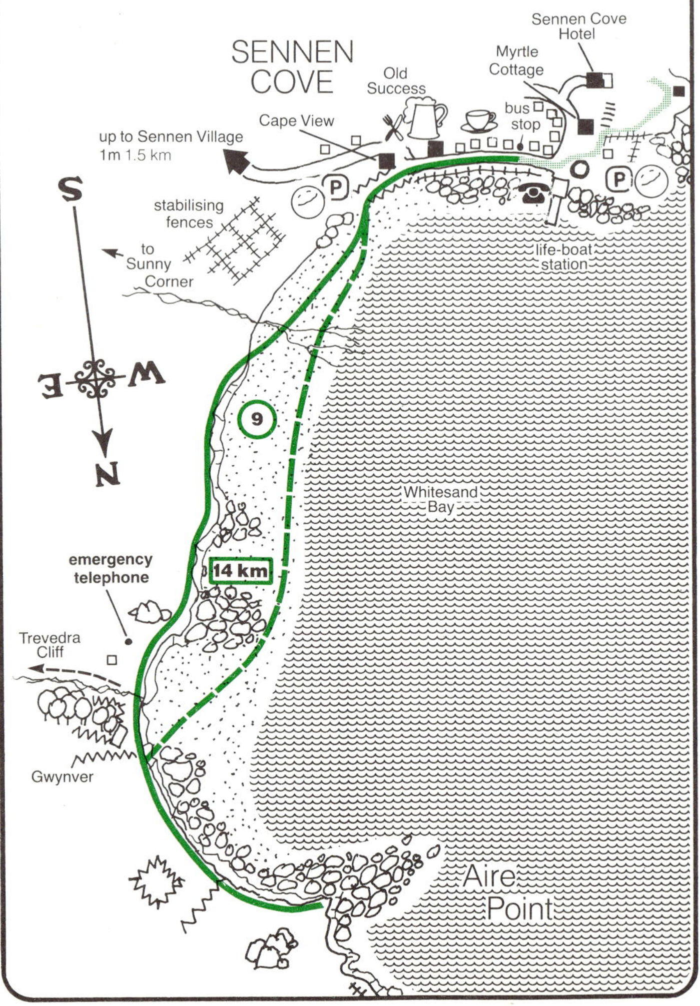

Aire Point to Sennen Cove

Going: Sennen Cove is just across the bay. If the tide is going out, walk across the beach, otherwise take the easy path along the cliff edge.

The path follows the cliff edge, just above the beach. From Aire Point you can see the whole stretch of the bay with Sennen Cove at the far end. Behind Sennen Cove is Land's End. Three miles *5 km* across the bay from here, and just over a mile from Land's End stands Longships Lighthouse.

The first Longships Lighthouse, on the Carn Bras rocks, was built in 1795. The first keepers had a hard life and there were many stories of madness and hair turning white overnight. A lovely local story relates how a keeper was kidnapped by wreckers, who failed to discover his tiny daughter. They were foiled by the brave little maiden, who every night stood on the family Bible to light the lamps until relief came. In 1873 a new lighthouse was built, with a lamp that could be seen for $17\frac{1}{2}$ miles *28 km*.

At Gywnver, a short cut can be taken to Sennen Cove across the beach, providing the tide is well out, or is going out.

You might like to know the state of the tide during your Footpath-Touring. Most national daily papers include in their Weather columns times of high and low tides at London Bridge. By adding three hours to these, reasonably accurate tide times are obtained. Both *The Times* and the *Daily Telegraph* not only give high tide times for Penzance and Falmouth, but they include the heights in metres too!

The fine long beach of Whitesand Bay only gets crowded close to Sennen Cove, even during the height of the season. Dangerous currents make swimming unsafe, but close to Sennen Cove these currents are less tricky, and there are usually life-guards on duty from May to September.

Near the stream that flows down from Sunny Corner, an attempt is being made to stabilise the sand dunes by fencing and planting marram grass.

Enter Sennen Cove by the ramp between the car park and the white-painted Old Success Inn.

The Old Success is said to get its name from its popularity among the smugglers as a place to celebrate successful operations.

There has been a lifeboat station at Sennen Cove since 1853. Today the lifeboat can claim to have saved almost 200 lives. Visitors are welcomed here most days.

Near the lifeboat station is a circular wooden building which once provided cover for a man-powered capstan which hauled in fishing-boats. Recently it has been used as a store for nets.

History has been here. King Arthur was said to have beaten off a Viking invasion near this beach, and in 1646, the young Prince Charles sailed from here on his escape from England, when the King surrendered to Parliament.

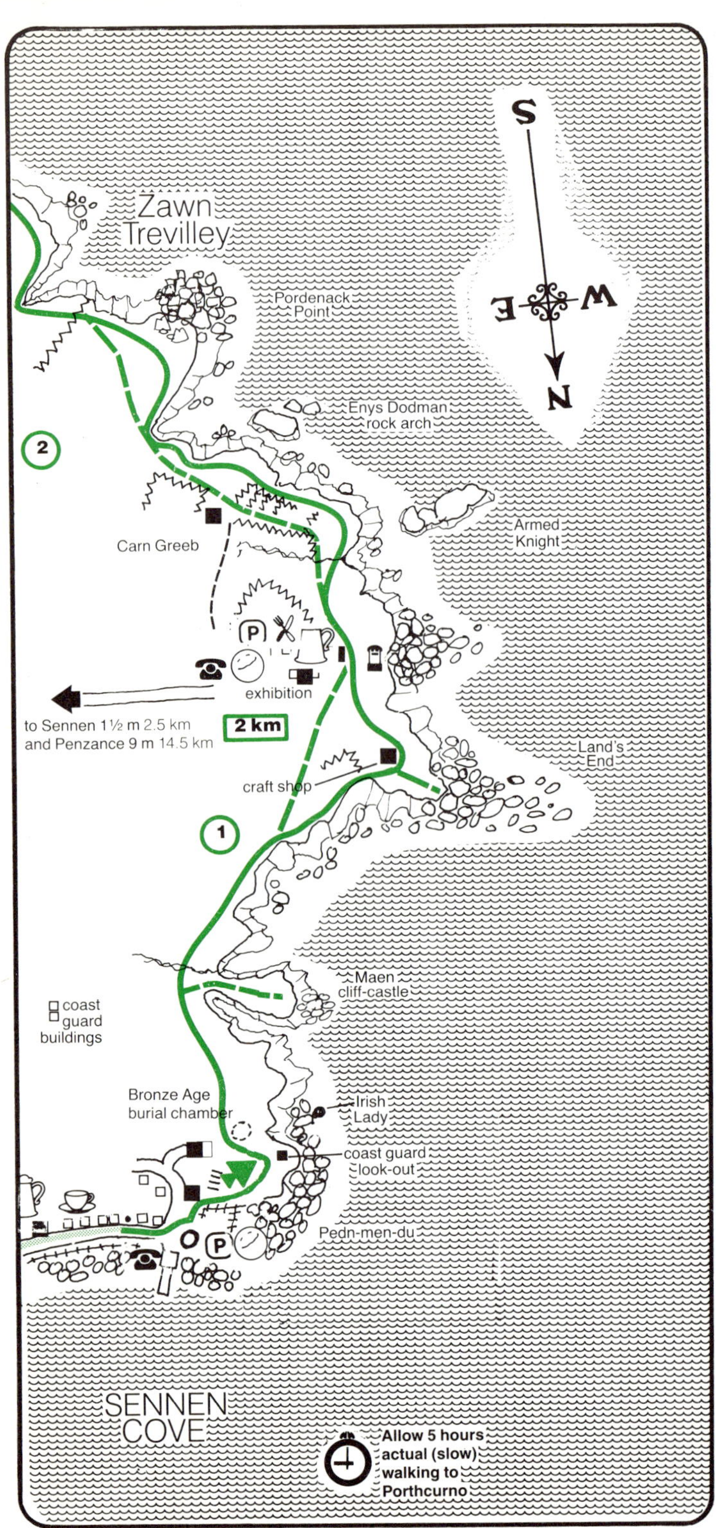

S
W
E
N
Zawn Trevilley
Pordenack Point
Enys Dodman rock arch
2
Carn Greeb
Armed Knight
P
exhibition
to Sennen 1½ m 2.5 km
and Penzance 9 m 14.5 km
2 km
Land's End
craft shop
1
Maen cliff-castle
coast guard buildings
Bronze Age burial chamber
Irish Lady
coast guard look-out
P
Pedn-men-du
SENNEN COVE
Allow 5 hours actual (slow) walking to Porthcurno

Lunch From Sennen Cove to Land's End should take about an hour. Land's End to Porthcurno, at a slow dawdle, should take about four hours.

At Land's End the State House cafeteria, with bar adjacent, welcome walkers. Open every day from mid March to end of October. So either make a late start and take early lunch at Land's End, or carry a picnic lunch to be taken somewhere around Mill Bay.

Sennen Cove to Zawn Trevilley

Going: One of the most spectacular stretches of Britain's coastline.

Leave Sennen Cove by western car park, and old Trinity House store with crest over the door. Climb track up to Coastguard look-out hut on Pedn-mên-du.

These magnificent cliffs of castellated granite are beloved by climbers, who can often be found down to the Right, just before the hut. Down to the left of the hut, a distinctive rock sticks up out of the sea, sometimes called The Irish Lady. Immediately on the Right of the most seaward track can be discovered the stone circles of a Bronze Age Burial chamber.

There are many alternative tracks that may be taken, but the most rewarding are those that meander nearest the sea.

An interesting detour will take you a few paces to the Right to explore Maen Cliff Çastle

Maen is Cornish for 'men'. This castle, dates from about 400 BC. Remains of defensive ditches and walls can be seen.

The most seaward path goes round to The First and Last House, now a craft shop. Walk down to look at the wild rocks of Land's End, the most westerly point of England.

Land's End (in Cornish, Pedn an Laaz – 'end of the earth') is a landmark known to seamen for centuries. It has long been the inspiration for artists, writers, and travellers, and is best seen in high winds, when furious waves lash the tumbled granite. From here America lies over 3000 miles *5000 km* across the Atlantic, and it is 874 miles *1400 km* to John o'Groat's, the most northerly point of mainland Britain.

Visitors arriving by road pay an entrance fee to the area, however you have right of way along the coast path, and the management insist that walkers are most welcome.

An excellent exhibition includes sections on birds, plants, archeology, Land's End 300 000 000 years ago, Man and the Sea, wrecks, rescues, and lighthouses. Small admission charge at door.

From the car park the seaward path again presents the most rewarding route.

The yellow cottage at Carn Greeb, on the Left of the path, marks where prehistoric man had a 'factory' producing knives, and arrowheads from 'imported' flints, for distribution over a wide area.

The rock island, Armed Knight, gets its name from its shape. Enys Dodman rock arch is a nesting-place for screeching Great Black-backed Gulls.

At Zawn Trevilley; be certain to look back at the 200 feet *60 m* cliffs of Pordenack Point. Zawn is Cornish for 'cliff chasm'.

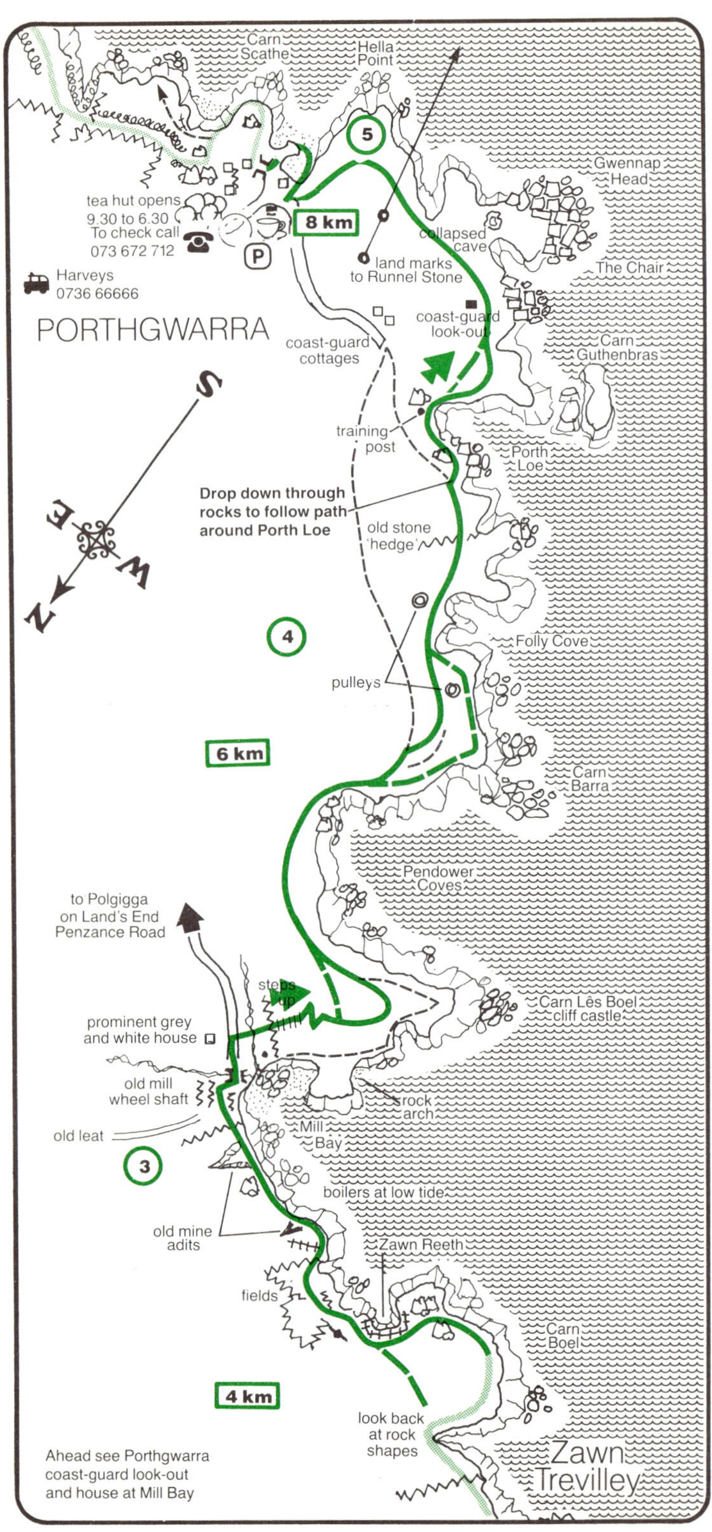
Carn Scathe
Hella Point
5
Gwennap Head
tea hut opens 9.30 to 6.30
To check call 073 672 712
8 km
collapsed cave
P
land marks to Runnel Stone
The Chair
Harveys 0736 66666
PORTHGWARRA
coast-guard look-out
coast-guard cottages
Carn Guthenbras
S
training post
Porth Loe
Drop down through rocks to follow path around Porth Loe
E
W
old stone 'hedge'
N
4
Folly Cove
pulleys
6 km
Carn Barra
Pendower Coves
to Polgigga on Land's End Penzance Road
steps up
Carn Lês Boel cliff castle
prominent grey and white house
old mill wheel shaft
rock arch
old leat
Mill Bay
3
boilers at low tide
old mine adits
Zawn Reeth
fields
Carn Boel
4 km
look back at rock shapes
Ahead see Porthgwarra coast-guard look-out and house at Mill Bay
Zawn Trevilley

Zawn Trevilley to Porthgwarra

Going: A superb walk with many short cuts, but the finest walking is to be found on the paths most seaward.

From Zawn Trevilley follow the path round the cliffs of Carn Boel, or take short cut across to the fenced cliffs at Zawn Reeth.

This zawn has had its moment of history (see page 62).

After crossing small walled fields, where daffodils can be found in the spring, a narrow cliff-edge path passes by openings to old adits.

At low tide you may see, just below the path, rusting boilers of the *City of Cardiff*, wrecked in 1912; all aboard being taken off by breeches-buoy.

Before the footbridge at Mill Bay (old name Nanjizel), look to the Left for the remains of the old mill-wheel shaft.

Turn Right off wide track to cross stream and climb steep steps towards Carn Lês Boel Cliff Castle. The cliff path gives fine views back across Mill Bay.

At the stream running down into Pendower Coves, bluebells can sometimes be found to the right.

There is a choice of routes over Carn Barra, but seaward is most spectacular.

Note the two pulleys set into the ground by Folly Cove, and speculate upon their purpose. They date from the Second World War. (Answer later.)

At Porth Loe, avoid a path bearing Left towards Coast-Guard Cottages. The correct route squeezes through boulders to drop down towards training post.

The post is used in exercises in the use of a breeches-buoy.

In 1905 the Liverpool ship *Khyber* was wrecked here with the loss of all but three of her twenty-six-man crew.

Climb steeply up to manned Coastguard look-out.

This lonely post was once an extremely busy station where operators were in constant communication with American Coastguards across the Atlantic. The operation is now housed in a large centre at Falmouth. If the Coastguard is not busy, you will find he is very willing to tell you something about the vital work of the service. Give him a wave anyway!

The cliffs of Gwennap Head contain a well-known climb called The Chair. There is also an impressive hole formed by a collapsed sea cave. If searching for either, do so with great care.

On the Left of the path, two large cones, one black and white, one red, indicate to mariners the line on which the Runnel Stone lies, almost 1 mile *1·5 km* off the shore.

This hidden rock is said to have claimed forty vessels between the years 1880 and 1910. However, in 1923 the 6000-ton *City of Westminster* smashed off the top, so it now lurks 20 feet *6 m* below the waves. You can see the mast of the buoy marking the spot. You may also hear the melancholy moan when the wind is high enough to blow the buoy's organ-pipe warning.

The attractive path drops easily down into the fishing hamlet of Porthgwarra.

Chantilly House ☐
no evening meal
073 672 771

Mrs Pattemore ☐
no evening meal
073 672 712

Porthcurno House ☐
073 672 427

Grey Gables ☐
073 672 421

Mariner's Lodge ☐
073 672 236

Treen Farm ☐
see page 22
073 672 253

Treen Campsite ☐
see page 22
073 672 526

Logan Rock Inn (NT) ☐
1 m by footpath
see page 22

see map

see map

Harvey's
0736 66666

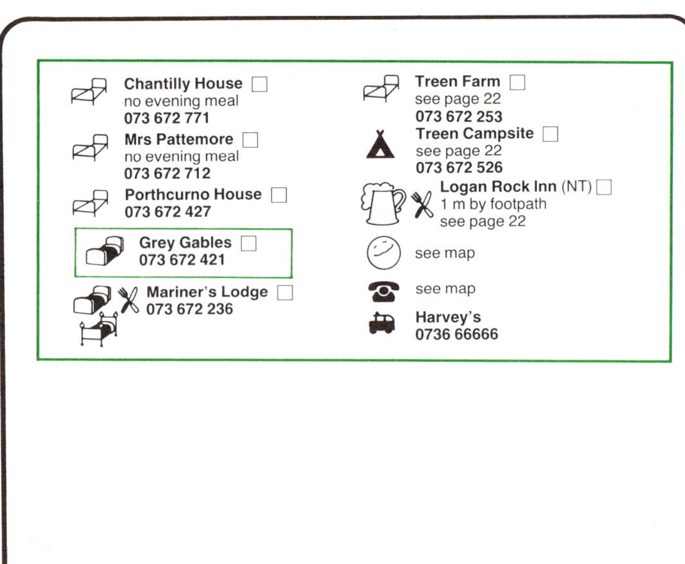

N
E
W
S
PORTHCURNO
PO
Chantilly
Mrs
Pattemore
Porthcurno
House
Mariner's
Lodge
10 km
Minack
theatre
metal
cage
Rospletha
Cliffs
6
Pedn-men-
an-mere
NT
Porth Chapel
emergency telephone
St. Levan
baptistry
Grey Gables
field
Carn
Barges
bear Right
to Carn Barges
unless visiting
St. Levan
field
Vessacks
field
Porthgwarra
Carn
Scathe
Allow 1 hours
actual walking
time to
Porthcurno
Hella
Point

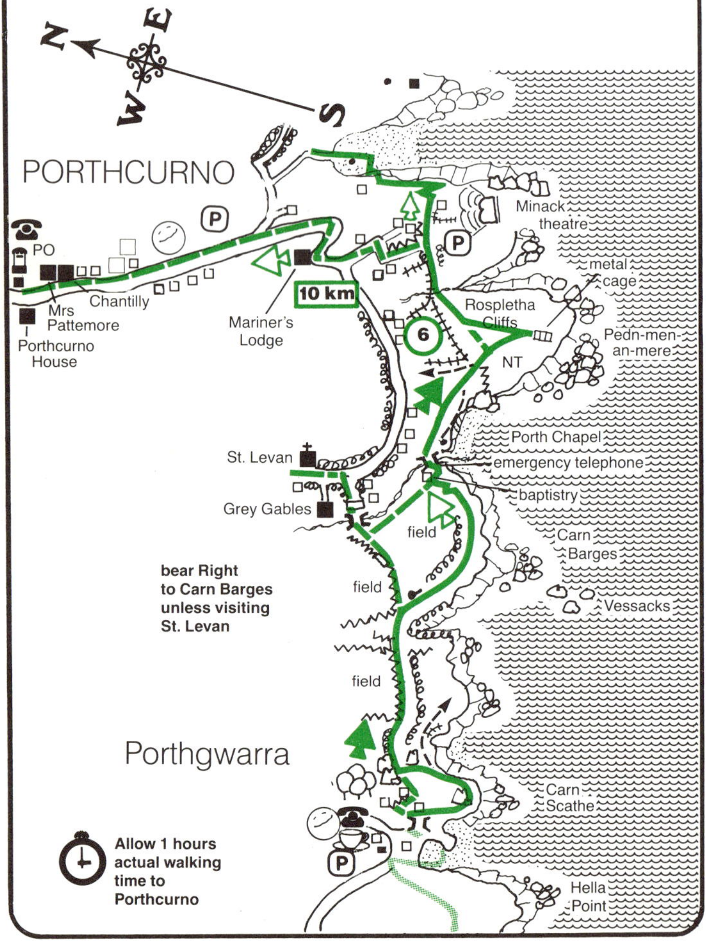

Porthgwarra to Porthcurno

Going: An enchanting walk, with superb sea views.

Porthgwarra is a handful of cottages said to have been established by families from a Breton fishing village. A tunnel cut through rock allows fishing-boats to be hauled in when the steep, cobbled slipway is pounded by heavy seas.

Coast path signs direct you between cottages, but a more interesting way is round the small headland of Carn Scathe.

Now the route, a little back from the cliff edge, climbs up a steep, boulder-stepped path, to give a high-level walk, with walled fields on the Left.

Note that the route follows the cliff edge round Carn Barges. Only proceed ahead if you are visiting St Levan Church or staying at the old rectory, Grey Gables.

St Levan is a corruption of Seleven, the 7thC Saint who is said to have landed at Porthchapel beach. The present church dates from the 13thC.

A stone in the churchyard mentions the loss of the *Khyber* (see page 19) while a large boulder split into two is called St Levan's stone. In the church, bench ends portray figures in medieval costume. A brass plate on the lectern contains a typographical error!

At the top of ancient stone steps stands St Levan's Baptistery, now a murky pool with a stone-wall surround. It is said that water from here is still used for some local Christening ceremonies.

By the red life-saving box, turn Left along the cliff-top path. On the other hand, if you have time to spare, and it is warm enough for a bathe, down on pleasant Porthchapel beach is as pleasant a spot as any.

Climb up to the headland of Pedn-mên-an-mere (NT).

A detour on to the headland will take you to a rusting cylindrical cage surrounded by iron rings embedded in concrete blocks. (See page 62 for its story.)

Follow fence on Left up into the car park of the Minack Theatre.

Minack is a spectacular open-air theatre, with seats cut into the sides of the cliff, and with the sea of the English Channel as a backdrop. The construction was very largely the physical handiwork of the remarkable Miss Rowena Cade. Shakespeare's *The Tempest* provided an ideal play for the first performance in 1932. Since then the theatre has grown in size and fame. I was once sheltering from windswept rain under a bush in the theatre drive when the frail Miss Cade, not sheltering, came by and insisted I join her indoors for a coffee.

A small sum placed in a collecting-box, gains admission to look.

Performances are confined to the summer. For details of programmes and times telephone 073 672 471. Take something warm to sit upon and something warmer to wear.

Continue beyond the theatre to descend to Porthcurno beach by precipitous steps, also the work of Miss Cade with her trowel. A less hazardous descent may be made down by the road into Porthcurno village.

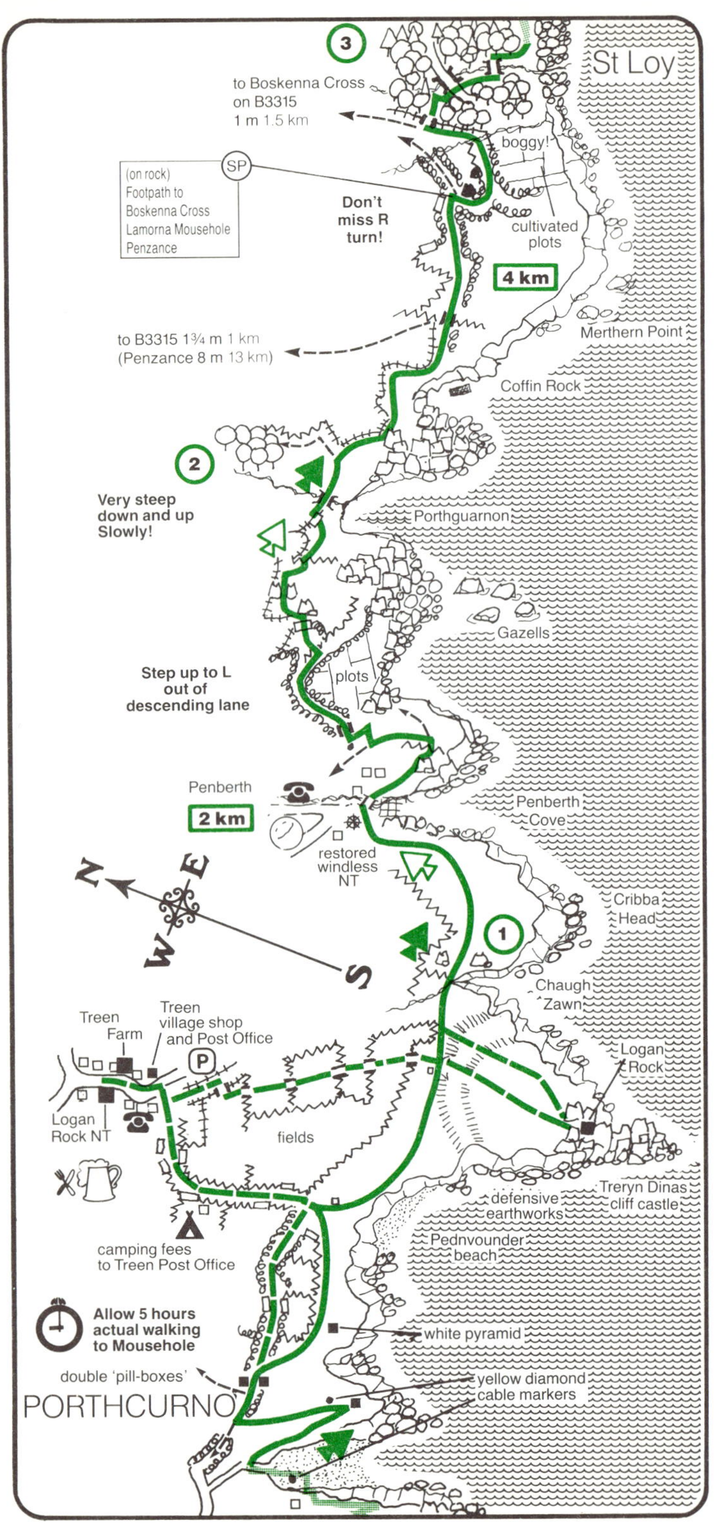
3
St Loy
to Boskenna Cross
on B3315
1 m 1.5 km
SP
(on rock)
Footpath to
Boskenna Cross
Lamorna Mousehole
Penzance
boggy!
Don't
miss R
turn!
cultivated
plots
4 km
Merthern Point
to B3315 1¾ m 1 km
(Penzance 8 m 13 km)
Coffin Rock
2
Very steep
down and up
Slowly!
Porthguarnon
Gazells
Step up to L
out of
descending lane
plots
Penberth
2 km
Penberth
Cove
restored
windless
NT
N
E
W
S
Cribba
Head
1
Chaugh
Zawn
Treen
Farm
Treen
village shop
and Post Office
P
Logan
Rock
Logan
Rock NT
fields
Treryn Dinas
cliff castle
defensive
earthworks
camping fees
to Treen Post Office
Pednvounder
beach
Allow 5 hours
actual walking
to Mousehole
white pyramid
double 'pill-boxes'
yellow diamond
cable markers
PORTHCURNO

Lunch may be taken at Lamorna Cove (see page 25.)

Porthcurno to St Loy

Going: A walk with many ups and downs, but magnificent coastal scenery.

The beach at Porthcurno is composed of fragments of white sea shells, which gives the sea a distinctive blue-green colour. Parts of the BBC television's 'Poldark', series were filmed here.

Porthcurno is a name well known in the field of communications, and students from all over the world attend the Cable and Wireless Engineering College. Porthcurno was also an important terminus for submarine telegraph cables that connected England with the Empire. The first cable to India, laid in 1870, entered the sea off this beach. Sometimes high winds uncover remains of the twenty-one cables once buried here.

Leave beach to climb up to wartime pill-box on cliffs, where turn Left. Turn Right on to walled lane. Shortly after double pill-box, take Right fork on to path past white pyramid.

The pyramid was erected by the National Trust to replace an old shed which had become a landmark for mariners. The shed originally marked the site where the first transatlantic cable was brought ashore in 1880.

By a National Trust collecting-box, walled lane leads into the village of Treen.

Continue on cliff path. A gap in high earthworks on Right marks detour down to the Iron Age cliff castle of Treryn Dinas, with its series of bank and ditch defences.

Among the rocks and boulders lies the famous Logan rocking-stone, which was toppled into the sea by Lieutenant Goldsmith of the Royal Navy. Public indignation obliged him to replace the stone at his own expense. (See list of costs in Treen pub.)

Down to Chaugh Zawn and up to cross gorse-covered Cribba Head. Drop down into the photogenic hamlet of Penberth.

The splendidly preserved hand capstan once hauled fishing-boats up the slip. The modern-day power comes from a noisy little motor in a shed.

Up out of Penberth, and turn sharp Left on headland. Aim for television aerial that protrudes above bushes, and turn Right on to a hedged lane. By cultivated plots on Right, do not miss step up on Left, to cross field up to gate. A certain amount of negotiation brings you to the top of the path that drops steeply down to cross stream at Porthguarnon. Care needed if path is wet and slippery. Steeply up, and Right at fence at top.

From Coffin Rock, seen down at bottom of cliff, path loses sight of the sea behind Merthen Point. On entering hedged lane, look for Right turn, indicated by painted rocks.

Behind cliff-edge cultivated plots, negotiate an often boggy corner, and in few yards cross stile on Right into spinney.

Drop down through trees, cross private drive, and muddily emerge on to boulder-strewn beach of St Loy.

Sheltered St Loy has reputation of being one of the warmest spots in England, and often makes a sunny coffee stop. An Early Christian chapel once stood here.

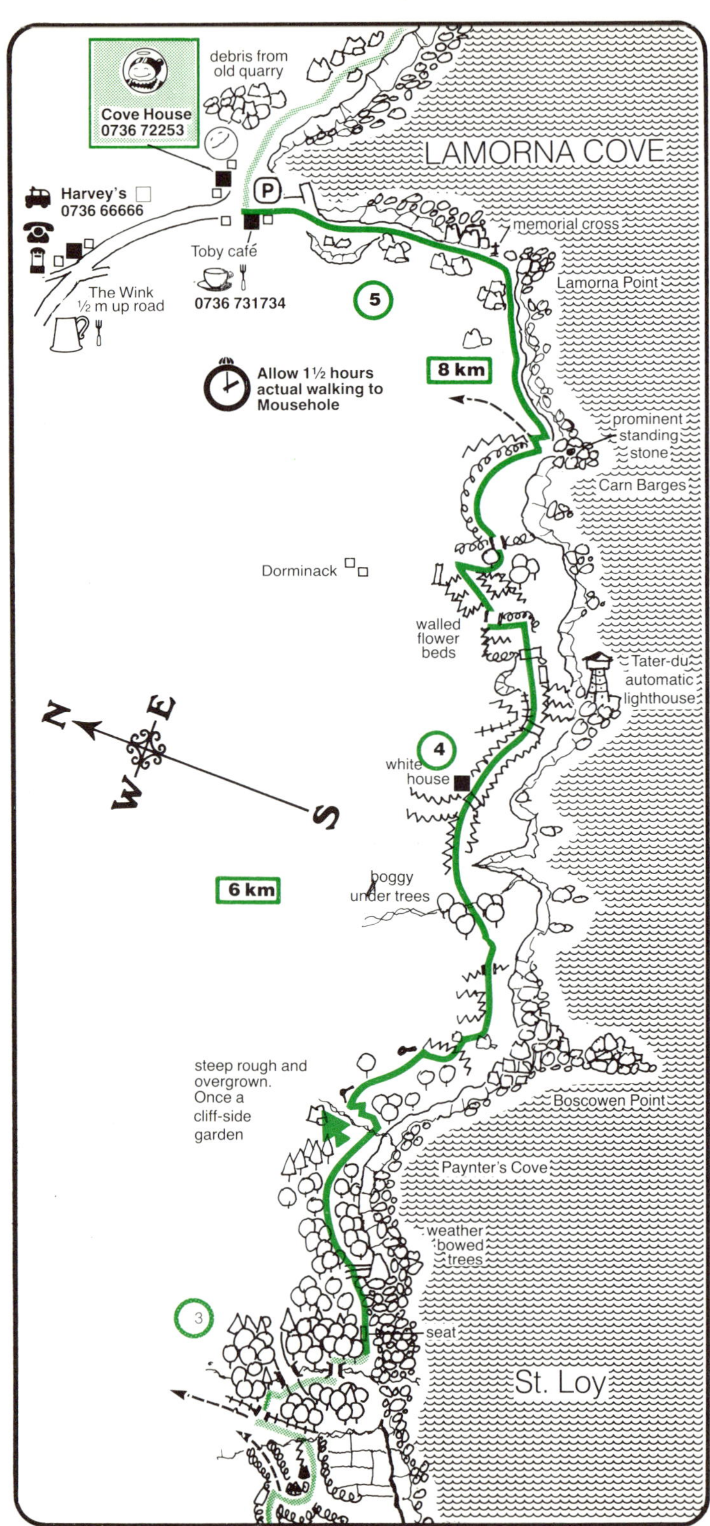
debris from
old quarry
Cove House
0736 72253
LAMORNA COVE
Harvey's
0736 66666
P
memorial cross
Toby café
0736 731734
Lamorna Point
The Wink
½ m up road
5
8 km
Allow 1½ hours
actual walking to
Mousehole
prominent
standing
stone
Carn Barges
Dorminack
walled
flower
beds
Tater-du
automatic
lighthouse
N
E
W
S
4
white
house
6 km
boggy
under trees
steep rough and
overgrown.
Once a
cliff-side
garden
Boscowen Point
Paynter's Cove
weather
bowed
trees
3
seat
St. Loy

St Loy to Lamorna Cove

Going: A little forbearance is required for this stretch, which is not the Countryside Commission's best testimonial for long-distance path-making. The luxurious growth everywhere is quite different from the bare headlands round Land's End.

Proceed behind beach, then with sure-footed balancing act, enter gap behind earth shoulder, beneath wind-bowed trees.

At Paynter's Cove fight up through vegetation which was once a cliff-side garden – it can be hard work.

Path eases at Boscowen Point. After boggy patch beneath trees enter walled lane.

It was just off the coast here that the *Union Star* foundered in December 1981 resulting in the death of all of the eight-man crew of the Penlee (near Mousehole) lifeboat.

At the time of writing, the white house by the gate is the home of John Le Carré of *Tinker, Tailor, Soldier, Spy*, and *Smiley's People*.

The walled lane leads past the track which drops steeply down to the Tater-du automatic lighthouse.

This was installed in 1965 after a series of shipwrecks off this section of coast. The light can be seen for 16 miles *26 km*. The fog-horn has a honeycomb of seventy-two speakers. This prominent white structure, low down below the cliff, will be visible when we are walking along the Lizard coast to Prah Sands.

The route, a bit contorted but easily followed, leads through the flower fields of author Derek Tangye.

Follow path, easily now, to Carn Barges standing stone, and drop down to cliff-edge path to Lamorna Point.

A stone cross commemorates a Cambridge student who fell to his death in 1873.

Negotiate boulder-strewn path into Lamorna Cove.

The little harbour at Lamorna Cove is often busy with fishing- and pleasure-boats.

The granite pier was built to ship stone from the now-abandoned quarry that litters the far side of the cove. This silver-grey stone was in much demand and was used all over England for over a hundred years. The old Waterloo Bridge was built of it.

Lamorna Cove has a pleasant café which is open every day, Easter to October.

Ten minutes up the pleasant lane, through alder and hazel, brings you to The Wink pub (note the pub sign.) The name stems back to the time when anyone could open an alehouse on payment of £20. The sale of spirits was not allowed. However a wink at the landlord would invariably result in the appearance of a brandy that had probably fallen off the back of a smuggler's lugger. Bar snacks are available throughout the year.

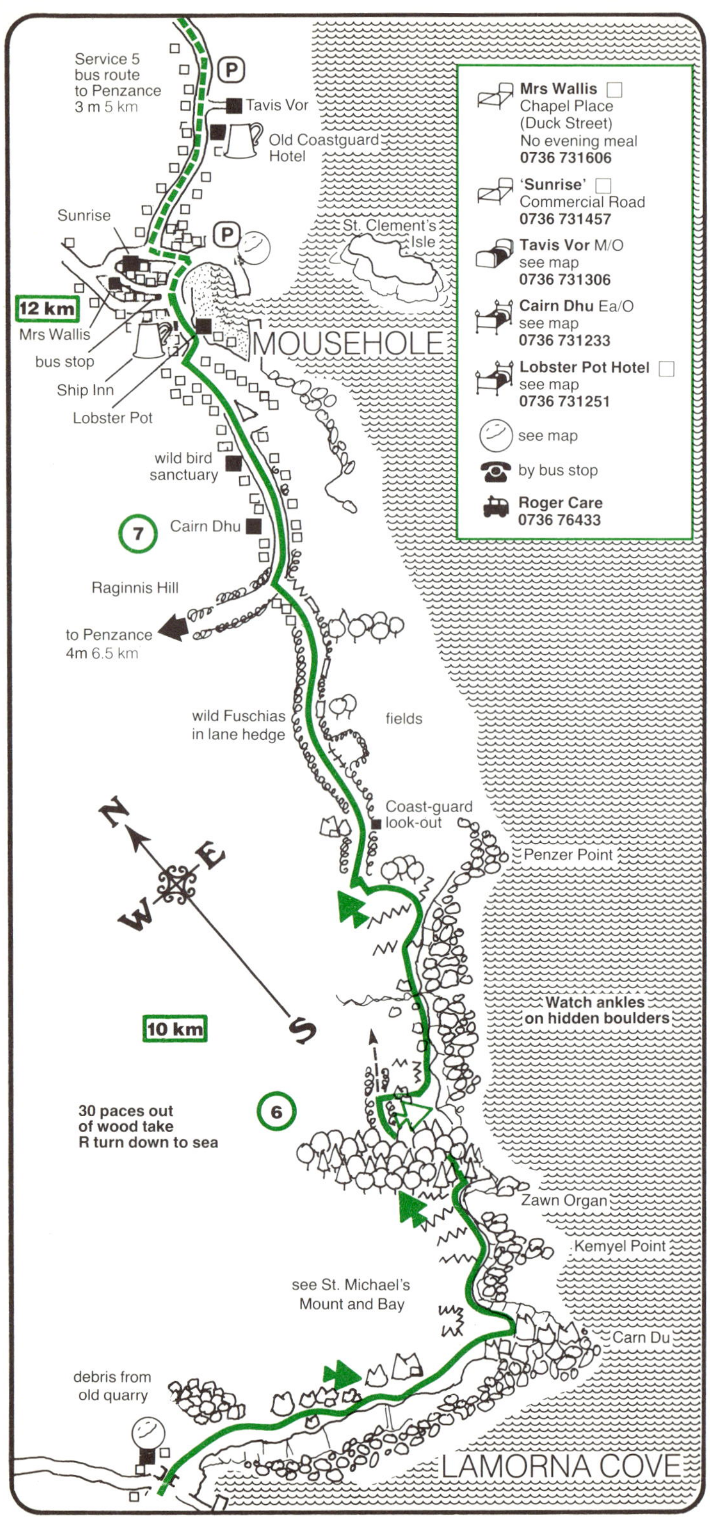

Service 5
bus route
to Penzance
3 m 5 km
Tavis Vor
Old Coastguard
Hotel
Sunrise
St. Clement's
Isle
12 km
Mrs Wallis
bus stop
Ship Inn
Lobster Pot
MOUSEHOLE
wild bird
sanctuary
7
Cairn Dhu
Raginnis Hill
to Penzance
4m 6.5 km
wild Fuschias
in lane hedge
fields
Coast-guard
look-out
Penzer Point
N
E
W
S
Watch ankles
on hidden boulders
10 km
30 paces out
of wood take
R turn down to sea
6
Zawn Organ
Kemyel Point
see St. Michael's
Mount and Bay
Carn Du
debris from
old quarry
LAMORNA COVE
Mrs Wallis
Chapel Place
(Duck Street)
No evening meal
0736 731606
'Sunrise'
Commercial Road
0736 731457
Tavis Vor M/O
see map
0736 731306
Cairn Dhu Ea/O
see map
0736 731233
Lobster Pot Hotel
see map
0736 731251
see map
by bus stop
Roger Care
0736 76433

Lamorna Cove to Mousehole

Going: A pleasant coastal walk, followed by a lane which leads easily down into Mousehole Harbour.

The path climbs through quarry debris to the headland of Carn-du.

From here you have a fine view over Mounts Bay and St Michael's Mount, looking like a fairy castle island. Away in the distance can be seen the houses of Marazion, and the long line of the Lizard coast. If the sun catches them, you can often see the large dish aerials of the Goonhilly satellite tracking station.

Drop down to walk just above the shore, past Kemyel Point.

At Zawn Organ the path climbs up, inland, briefly through rather gloomy fir trees. Just out of the wood, turn Right, down boulder steps, to rejoin the shore-line path.

This is a rough section of path, so place your feet carefully.

It was here that the £1 000 000 freezer trawler *Conqueror* from Hull ran aground late in 1977. Within days £25 000 worth of equipment disappeared from the wreck, and salvage attempts were abandoned!

Climb steeply up to the Coastguard look-out behind Penzer Point.

This makes a splendid spot to rest. There is even a stone armchair. Fine views over the bay from this 225 feet *69 m* eyrie.

A hedged lane now leads to the road down into Mousehole (pronounced Mowzel).

One of the houses perched high up on the Left has become the Mousehole Bird Hospital where injured gulls, gannets, and cormorants are nursed back to health. You are welcome to visit in return for a small donation.

The road down gives a fine view over the Mousehole roof-tops. The tiny island of St Clement's once housed a small chapel dedicated to the Patron Saint of Seafarers.

Point Spaniard gets its name from an event in 1595 when 200 Spaniards from three galleons were said to have landed to pillage and burn the town. One of the buildings that survived was the Manor House in Keigwin Street, although squire Jenkin Keigwin was said to have been slain on the threshold. It has an impressive porch and small room supported on granite pillars. It eventually became a pub for a time. Recently the BBC used it as a location in their 'Poldark' series.

The Lobster Pot hotel has a quaint dining-room which protrudes out over the harbour.

The impressive pier was built in 1861.

In the holiday season Mousehole gets crowded, a situation which is aggravated by motorists who insist upon nosing along its narrow, twisting streets.

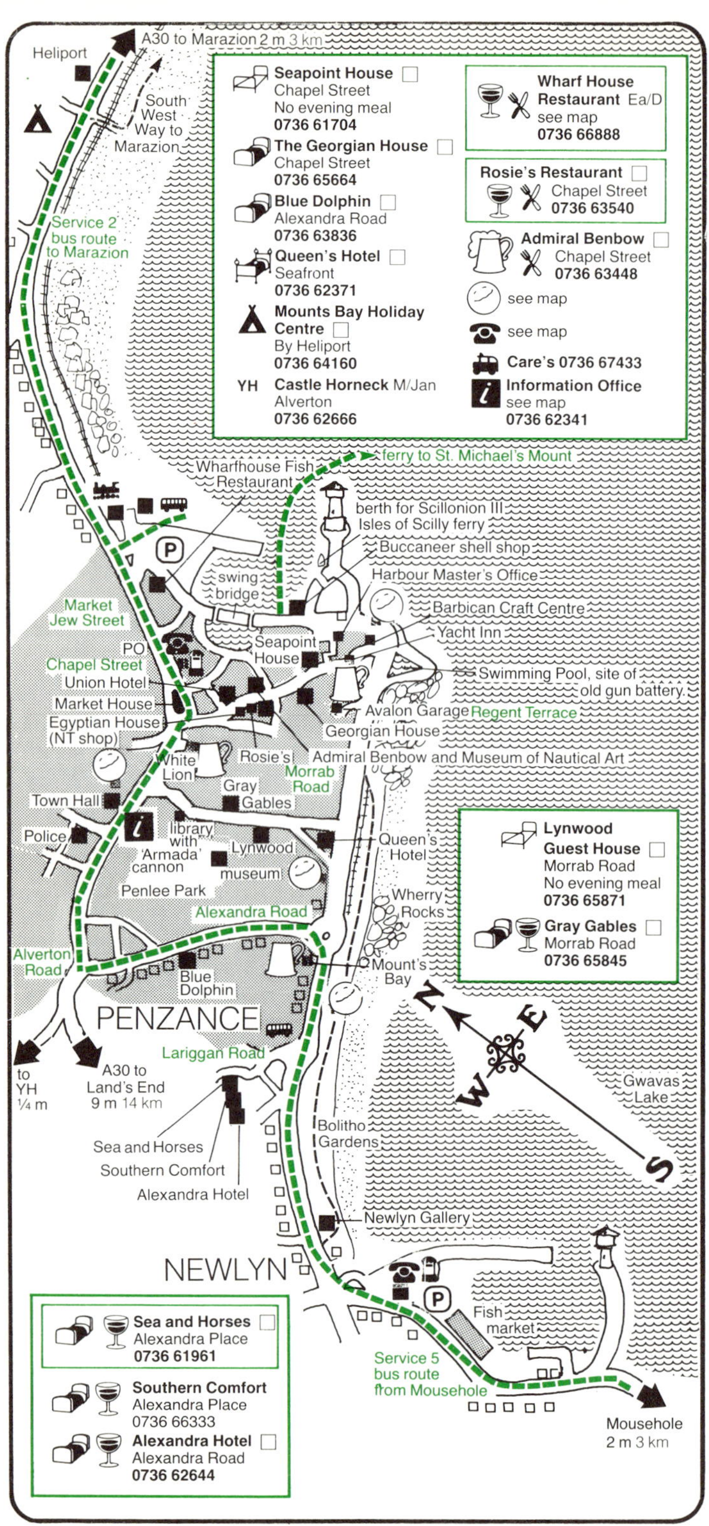

A30 to Marazion 2 m 3 km
Heliport
South West Way to Marazion
Service 2 bus route to Marazion
Seapoint House
Chapel Street
No evening meal
0736 61704
The Georgian House
Chapel Street
0736 65664
Blue Dolphin
Alexandra Road
0736 63836
Queen's Hotel
Seafront
0736 62371
Mounts Bay Holiday Centre
By Heliport
0736 64160
YH Castle Horneck M/Jan
Alverton
0736 62666
Wharf House Restaurant Ea/D
see map
0736 66888
Rosie's Restaurant
Chapel Street
0736 63540
Admiral Benbow
Chapel Street
0736 63448
see map
see map
Care's 0736 67433
Information Office
see map
0736 62341
ferry to St. Michael's Mount
Wharfhouse Fish Restaurant
berth for Scillonion III
Isles of Scilly ferry
Buccaneer shell shop
Harbour Master's Office
Barbican Craft Centre
Yacht Inn
swing bridge
Market Jew Street
PO
Chapel Street
Union Hotel
Market House
Egyptian House (NT shop)
Seapoint House
Swimming Pool, site of old gun battery
Avalon Garage
Regent Terrace
Georgian House
Admiral Benbow and Museum of Nautical Art
White Lion
Rosie's
Morrab Road
Gray Gables
Town Hall
Police
library with 'Armada' cannon
Lynwood
museum
Queen's Hotel
Penlee Park
Alexandra Road
Wherry Rocks
Lynwood Guest House
Morrab Road
No evening meal
0736 65871
Gray Gables
Morrab Road
0736 65845
Alverton Road
Blue Dolphin
Mount's Bay
PENZANCE
Lariggan Road
N
E
W
S
to YH ¼ m
A30 to Land's End 9 m 14 km
Gwavas Lake
Sea and Horses
Southern Comfort
Alexandra Hotel
Bolitho Gardens
Newlyn Gallery
NEWLYN
Fish market
Service 5 bus route from Mousehole
Mousehole 2 m 3 km
Sea and Horses
Alexandra Place
0736 61961
Southern Comfort
Alexandra Place
0736 66333
Alexandra Hotel
Alexandra Road
0736 62644

Lunch: Wide choice in Penzance.
We recommend: *Admiral Benbow*. Pub with décor which is extension of Museum of Nautical Art opposite. Good seafood snacks.

Rosie's. Informal bistro with warm welcome and good food.

The Wharfhouse Fish Restaurant. Excellent traditional 'fish and chip' menu. Fish comes from boats just down the road!

Mousehole to Penzance

Going: The Footpath-Touring route from Mousehole, through Newlyn, to Penzance makes use of public transport.

From the War Memorial by the Ship Inn, on the harbour, Service 5 buses leave Monday to Saturday throughout the year, at half-hour intervals. Journey takes twenty minutes. Enquiries to: Western National, telephone 0736 62274.

(It is possible to walk along by coast road, past the quarries, but it is unedifying and the time can be better spent in Penzance.)

Newlyn. Most important fishing port in West Country. Old pier of 1435 still stands. New harbour completed 1980. Fishing-boats often include crabbers and trawlers from Belgium and France.

Penzance. Once a major trading port, now dedicated mainly to holiday industry. Name comes from Pens Sans (means 'holy headland', and refers to ancient chapel which once stood above harbour). Lighthouse Pier is departure point for *Isles of Scilly*. Royal Mail Motor Vessel *Scillonian* leaves daily for two-and-a-half-hour journey, Scilly Steamship Co. (For details 0736 62009). Regular helicopter flights by British Airways take twenty minutes from Heliport. (For details telephone 0736 63871.)

Aircraft flights from Land's End Airport. A ten-minute flight along the coast will cost you less than £10. (For details telephone 0736 788771/788601.)

From Information Office obtain **Penzance Town Trail**, also free guide to **Chapel Street**, a street of Regency and Georgian houses. **Museum of Nautical Art** contains treasures lifted from sea bed by diver Roland Morris, and examples of shipbuilder's crafts. Fascinating full-size section of four-decker, 95-gun man-o'-war of about 1730. Open 10.00 hrs to 17.00 hrs, May to October. Also in Chapel Street, **Egyptian House**, built 1820 during wave of enthusiasm for all things Egyptian, and now a National Trust shop. Opposite, **Union Hotel** boasts musicians' gallery in dining-room, from where England first learned of Nelson's victory, and death, at *Trafalgar*. (Ask permission to see.)

Penzance Museum, Penlee House. Cornish antiquities. Excellent. Admission free. Open 10.30 hrs to 16.30 hrs.

Market House, with copper dome and Ionic columns, built 1828. In front, statue of **Sir Humphry Davy**, inventor of miner's safety-lamp, looks down street of his birthplace.

St Michael's Mount (NT), should be visited if schedule, weather, and tides permit. In 1044 Edward the Confessor built Benedictine Priory, perched 200 feet *60 m* above seas on this romantic-looking island. Magnificent 14thC castle is open April to May, Mondays, Wednesdays, Fridays. June to end October, Monday to Friday. Enquiries telephone 0736 710507. Ferry-boats leave from North Pier. Book at Buccaneer Shell Shop. Note: Winds and tides govern sailings, so always check (telephone 0736 62479).

PERRANUTHNOE
Victoria
0736 710309
S
E
N
W
1
spoil heap
fields
seat
The Greeb
Peranuthnoe ¾ m
SP
Peranuthnoe 1 m
Beach ½ m
SP
allotments
cemetery
Bolteron Road
Allow 2½ hours actual walking to Prah Sands
SP
Coastpath
Henfor Terrace
Mounts Bay
Shop Hill
School Lane
Wheal-an-wens
St. Michael's Mount (NT)
Cutty Sark
ferry
PO
causeway
MARAZION
P
route of service 2 bus from Penzance
Great Hogus
South West Way from Penzance
A394 to Penzance 3 m 5 km
Little Hogus
route of ferry from Penzance
If tides and weather permit, bus journey can be replaced by taking boat from Penzance to St. Michael's Mount, (see page 29) and then by causeway or local ferry to Marazion.
To check that Marazion ferry is operating, telephone National Trust, St Michael's Mount, 0736 710507.
Causeway is usually clear for walking 4 hours after High Tide, (see page 15) and remains clear for approximately 4 hours.

Lunch: Excellent snacks are available at the Victoria inn, Perranuthnoe. (See *both* sides of inn-sign!)

Otherwise carry a picnic lunch. There are several sheltered spots on the cliff edge, near Flavel's Hole, with magnificent sea views.

Penzance to Perranuthnoe

Going: The Footpath-Touring route uses public transport from Penzance to Marazion. (You could make the 3 mile *5 km* walk along road and beach, but the front seat on top of a double-decker bus is more rewarding.)

Service 2 leaves the bus station at 8.05 hrs, then about every hour. The journey takes about fifteen minutes. Ask to be put down at Marazion Cemetery! Enquiries telephone 0736 62274.

There follows a pleasant field walk from the outskirts of Marazion into the village of Perranuthnoe.

Marazion was once the resting-place for pilgrims heading for St Michael's Mount. Today it caters for tourists who take ferry-boats to the mount or, when the tide is right, walk the ¼ mile *0·5 km* stone causeway.

Mariners sailing from the English Channel to the Bristol Channel, would often bring their boats ashore on this beach, and haul them across the 4 mile *6·5 km* neck of land to St Ives, rather than face the dangers of the Land's End coast in bad weather.

In recent years motorists have had cause to complain of the bottle-neck presented by the narrow, twisting main street. A new by-pass, opened in 1984, eased this problem.

Immediately beyond Marazion Cemetery, enter the hedged lane and follow signposts for Perranuthnoe.

Although path is well inland you can usually plainly see the long finger of rocks, The Greeb, reaching out from the shore. There are also superb views back across Mounts Bay, and you should be able to pick out Mousehole, the quarry, Newlyn, and Penzance.

Cross farm lane and field. Look for Cornish stone stiles and follow hedges and wall on Left until entering lane at Perranuthnoe. Follow lane round to Right to church, then ahead to join main road through village. Victoria inn will be seen off to Left.

At the beginning of the 19thC several small copper-mines were grouped round the village, including Wheal Neptune, Wheal Charlotte, and Wheal Trebarvah.

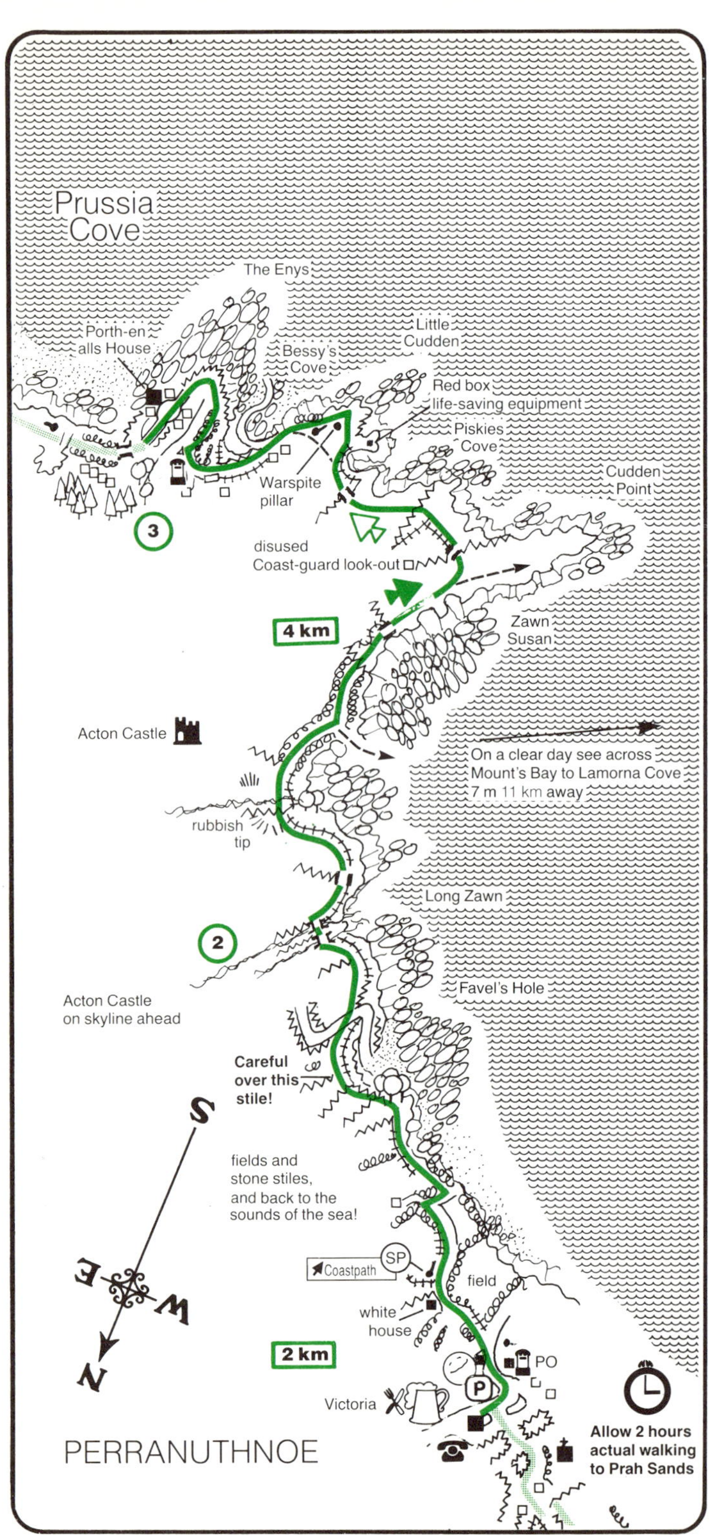
Prussia Cove
The Enys
Porth-en alls House
Little Cudden
Bessy's Cove
Red box life-saving equipment
Piskies Cove
Warspite pillar
Cudden Point
3
disused Coast-guard look-out
4 km
Zawn Susan
Acton Castle
On a clear day see across Mount's Bay to Lamorna Cove 7 m 11 km away
rubbish tip
Long Zawn
2
Favel's Hole
Acton Castle on skyline ahead
Careful over this stile!
fields and stone stiles, and back to the sounds of the sea!
S
E
W
N
Coastpath
SP
field
white house
2 km
PO
P
Victoria
Allow 2 hours actual walking to Prah Sands
PERRANUTHNOE

Perranuthnoe to Prussia Cove

Going: A very easy path, staying just behind beaches of boulders and rocks.

Leave Perranuthnoe by road leading down towards beach. At Post Office/shop fork Left along lane. At white house take Right fork down narrow hedged track. Do not go onto beach but follow cliff-edge path, now through fields and over stone stiles.

The path is lined in several places by the salt-breeze-loving Tamarisk, pretty evergreen shrub with feathery foliage, and clusters of tiny pink flowers.

Broad slabs of rock mark Favel's Hole.

The castellated building to be seen up on the Left is Acton Castle, built by an industrialist, and now sometimes a hotel.

The path heads towards Cudden Point, scene of many shipwrecks. Splendid coastal walking. At Piskies Cove take path that drops down to prominent wooden post on headland.

This pillar is a relic of one of the coast's many dramas. In 1947 the old 30 000-ton battleship HMS *Warspite*, veteran of two world wars, including the 1916 Battle of Jutland, was being towed ingloriously to a breaker's yard. A south-westerly gale blew up, and the old lady broke from her tugs and finished up on the rocks off this cove. The small crew on board were saved in an heroic and difficult rescue carried out by the men of Penlee lifeboat, over from Mousehole.

Hauling tackle was erected here so that heavy equipment could be taken off to lighten the ship for refloating. This post is all that remains of the hauling gear. *Warspite* was eventually moved, but again she broke loose to run ashore near St Michael's Mount. There she was finally broken up.

From the pillar do not climb back up to the higher path but find the sunken track which follows the cliff edge round to Bessy's Cove.

At Bessy's Cove a few fishermen can often be seen repairing nets, or making lobster-pots from Tamarisk switches. The cove gets its name from Bessy Burrows who ran an alehouse near here. This bit of coast with its coves and many caves was ideal for the smuggler.

The tracks in the flat black rocks which are revealed at low tide, were cut to allow carts to be loaded with seaweed, and then pulled by horses up to the fields where it was spread as fertiliser. The existing ramp down to the cove was cut after the Great Storm of 1891 washed a previous approach away, along with several fishing-boats.

The BBC filmed smuggling scenes here for their 'Poldark' series.

Past thatched cottage and post-box on Left, and up to turn Right on to wide drive.

Drive leads down to pass between the buildings of Porth-en-Alls House, at Prussia Cove.

The White House ☐
No evening meal
073 676 2329

Cara Del ☐
No evening meal
073 676 3438

Milford Haven ☐
No evening meal
073 676 3458

Prah Sands Hotel ☐
073 676 2438

Welloe Rock Inn ☐
073 676 3516

Clipper Fish and Chip Restaurant and Take Away ☐
073 676 3751

Higher Pentreath Farm Ea/O
073 676 3222

Camborne Information Office ☐
0209 712941

see map

see map

Paul's Cabs
073 676 2766

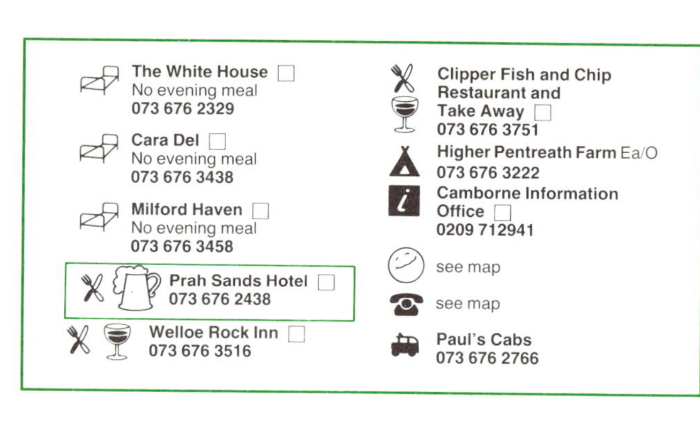

Up to A394
Marazion/Helston
road
¾ m 1 km
Milford
Haven
Prah
Sands
Hotel
PO
newsagent
and stores
White House
Cara Del
P
PRAH
SANDS
High Pentreath
Farm
Welloe
Rock Inn
Clipper
4
Hoe
Point
¾ m to A394
(Helston/Marazion
and Lower Kenneggy
Pestreath
Cove
Kenneggy
Cliff
6 km
S
E
N
W
track down
to Fine beach
Porth-en-alls
House
SP
Coastpath
old
quarry
Prussia Cove

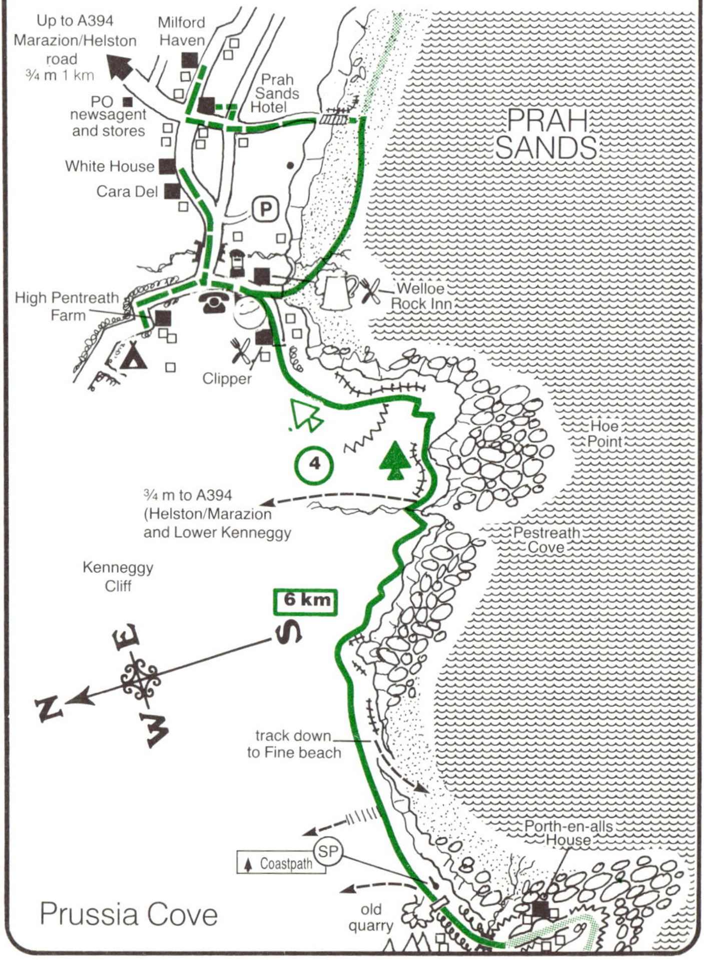

Prussia Cove to Prah Sands

Going: A delightful walk high above Keneggy beach, and a climb up to Hoe Point with spectacular views along the coast.

Leave Porth-en-Alls House by hedged lane, below 1820 Coastguard Cottages up on Left.

Porth-en-Alls House was built by the still-local Turnstall-Behrens family, although the beginning of the First World War prevented its final completion. Today it is let as holiday flats. The site was once the home of the successful 18thC smuggler John Carter.

John was nicknamed 'King of Prussia' by his brothers when still a young boy. The name stayed, and resulted in this cove becoming known as Prussia Cove. John was a strange mixture; a fearless smuggler and first-class mariner, but God-fearing and honest. When one of his cargoes was seized by Revenue officers and locked away in Penzance Customs House, he organised a raid to recover his contraband, but scrupulously refrained from touching goods that were not his. Despite the hazards posed by the French Revolution and the little matter of the declaration of war between England and France, John, with his brothers, continued to 'trade' and outwit the Revenue men.

They had several craft built for them, including a 30-ton cutter with a crew of ten. A small battery of guns were mounted here on the cove, ostensibly to ward off French privateers. However there is a local story that one day, seeing one of their smuggling luggers chased into the cove by the Revenue cutter *Fairy*, John was moved to open fire.

Today all is peaceful here and the 'fair traders' have long gone. Nevertheless a twilight walk can prompt the dullest imagination to set ears straining for the sound of muffled oars and whispered orders. And is that a light down among the rocks . . .?

The path now follows the edge of the 100 foot *30 m* high Keneggy Cliffs that overlook the fine sandy beach below. There are several little diversions where crumbling cliffs have taken the old path away, but it is all easy walking.

At Pestreath Cove, cross the little stream which seems to change its course after every heavy rainfall.

The path now climbs up through gorse above Hoe Point. There are good views over the holiday village of Prah Sands, with its 1 mile *1·5 km* long beach of clean firm sand.

Descend easily to Prah Sands beach. Pub and seasonable snack-bars.

Note that the Ordnance Survey use the spelling Prah Sands on their 1:25 000 series maps, and Praa Sands on their 1:50 000 series. Just to confuse further, the Cornish for common land is 'pras'.

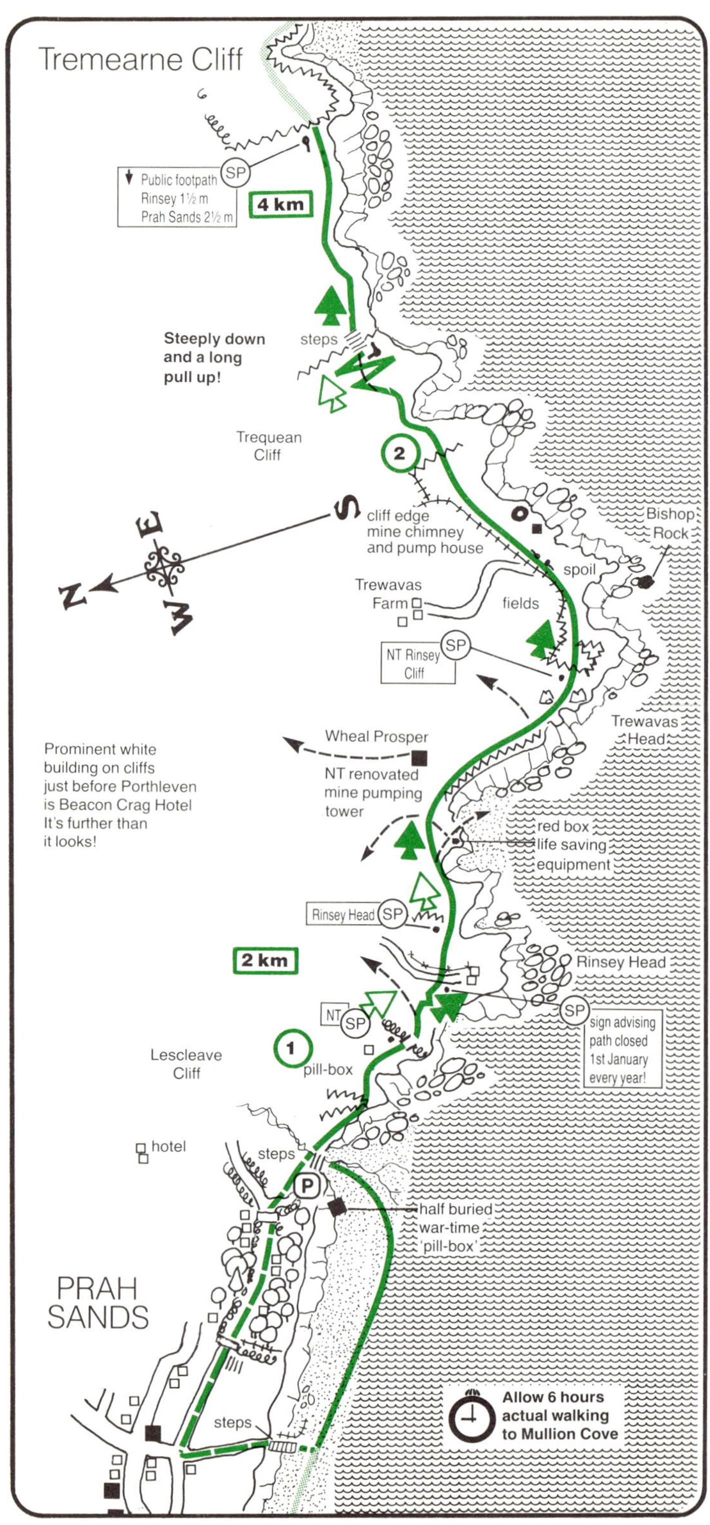
Tremearne Cliff
Public footpath
Rinsey 1½ m
Prah Sands 2½ m
SP
4 km
Steeply down
and a long
pull up!
steps
Trequean
Cliff
2
S
E
N
W
cliff edge
mine chimney
and pump house
Bishop
Rock
spoil
Trewavas
Farm
fields
NT Rinsey
Cliff
SP
Trewavas
Head
Wheal Prosper
NT renovated
mine pumping
tower
Prominent white
building on cliffs
just before Porthleven
is Beacon Crag Hotel
It's further than
it looks!
red box
life saving
equipment
Rinsey Head
SP
2 km
Rinsey Head
NT
SP
sign advising
path closed
1st January
every year!
1
Lescleave
Cliff
pill-box
hotel
steps
P
half buried
war-time
'pill-box'
PRAH
SANDS
steps
Allow 6 hours
actual walking
to Mullion Cove

Lunch: This is quite a long day and the attractive fishing harbour of Porthleven makes an excellent lunch stop.

Prah Sands to Tremearne Cliffs

Going: A beach walk leads to a fine cliff path with many ups and downs.

The day begins along the splendid beach. Walking is often easier down on the wet sand at the water's edge. (In unpleasant weather there is a more protected route along a drive serving holiday houses, which runs parallel to the beach. Despite 'Private' notices, there is a right of way.)

At eastern end of beach, by half-buried pill-box, steps lead up through cleft in cliffs.

Cliff path climbs Lescleave Cliff (NT).

Push through gorse, and cross bracken-filled hollow to go over private drive at Rinsey Head.

Path follows cliffs above Porthcew beach and passes beneath prominent pump-house and chimney of Wheal Prosper Mine.

Wheal Prosper ceased production as a copper-mine in 1860. In 1970 the National Trust spent £4000 on restoring this stone, brick-topped chimney and typical pump-house, standing above a 600 foot *180 m* shaft.

The path follows a sunken track on cliff edge to Rinsey Cliff (NT). At stone walls on Trewavas Head, climb up to follow fence on Left, past spoil heaps of the old Wheal Trewavas Mine.

The prominent and curiously shaped pillar of rock is known locally as Bishop Rock.

Keep to the path here. The gorse hides shafts not properly covered. However I recommend that you make a small detour down to the chimney and pump-house that perch on the edge of the cliff, 200 feet *60 m* above the sea, in a setting equally as dramatic as the better-known Crown Mines of Botallack (page 11).

Lodes ran far out beneath the sea, and it was said that miners underground could hear the shingle moving about on the sea bed, just above their heads.

Local legend also says the mine was closed about 1850 when the sea broke into the workings during the annual dinner underground!

From here the path wanders clearly along the cliffs, although a bit tortuous at times. A new zigzag path has been cut to ease the steep slopes of the valley at Trequean. At Tremeane Cliff, the path becomes a pleasant walk down a grass field, to a stream at the bottom.

Ahead the houses of the lunch-stop harbour seem tantalisingly close, but there is some hard walking yet to do.

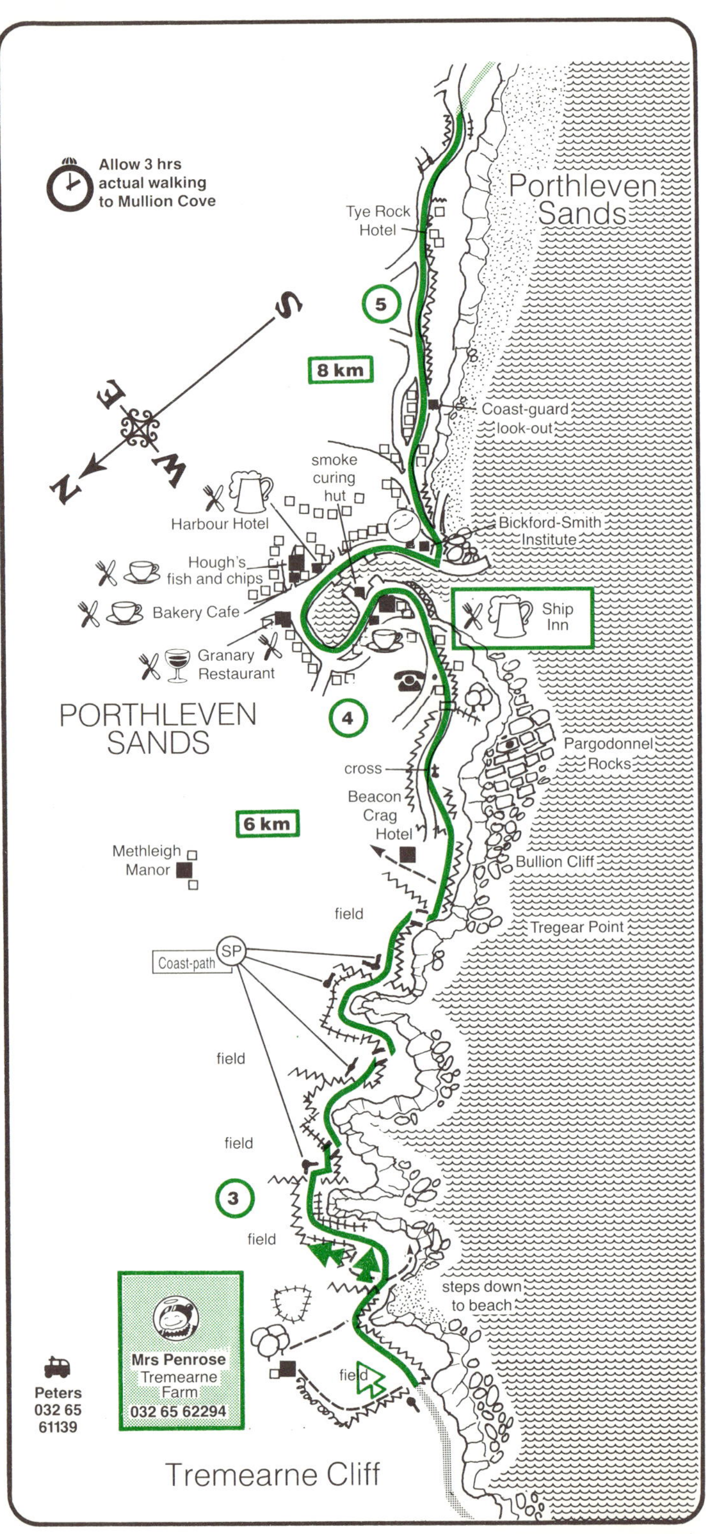
Allow 3 hrs actual walking to Mullion Cove
Porthleven Sands
Tye Rock Hotel
5
8 km
S
E
W
N
Coast-guard look-out
smoke curing hut
Harbour Hotel
Bickford-Smith Institute
Hough's fish and chips
Bakery Cafe
Ship Inn
Granary Restaurant
PORTHLEVEN SANDS
4
Pargodonnel Rocks
cross
Beacon Crag Hotel
6 km
Methleigh Manor
Bullion Cliff
field
Tregear Point
SP
Coast-path
field
field
3
field
steps down to beach
Mrs Penrose
Tremearne Farm
032 65 62294
Peters
032 65
61139
field
Tremearne Cliff

Tremearne Cliff to Porthleven Sands

Going: A path squeezed between cultivated fields and crumbling cliff edges. Fine sea views, even if the walking does go on a bit! The reward is a pleasant walk round Porthleven Harbour, with opportunity for rest and refreshment.

Continue to follow cliff edge, and resist the temptation to take short cuts across crops, as tracks suggest is sometimes done. The correct path is very clearly indicated with signs, sturdy fences, and stiles. (Thank you Cornwall County Council.)

There are said to be tunnels from the cliffs here to Methleigh Manor, a $\frac{1}{4}$ mile *0·5 km* inland. The manor kitchen had a hidden cellar in which contraband was once stored.

Just beyond Beacon Crag Hotel, route leaves cliff edge to join wide track.

The white cross on the Right is a reminder of the time when unidentified bodies washed up from the sea were not permitted to be buried in consecrated ground in case they should be heathen. About 100 yards *90 m* beyond the cross you can see below the cliffs a geological curiosity. Lodged in a rock pool on the flat platform of Pargodonnel Rocks is a large 10 feet *3 m* highly polished, brown boulder. This rock cannot be matched by any other rock in Britain, and is thought to have been stranded here by an iceberg during an Ice Age.

Pass through the Wrestling Field and join road, taking the Right fork down to the harbour of Porthleven.

The route goes all the way round the harbour to leave by the 70 feet *21 m* clock-tower opposite. (Note the splendid terrace of Victorian villas.)

The Ship Inn, standing on rock at the entrance to the harbour is over 200 years old and used to be called the Ship Tavern. It is said to have been a notorious place for smugglers. It is a good pub, patronised by the locals, and offering a very warm welcome. Bar snacks all through year.

Porthleven has long been a fishing village, once being known as Porth Leaven Cove.

In 1826 the granite harbour was built at a cost of £200 000. The inner-basin breakwater, with large baulks of timber that are dropped into place to keep out storms, dates from 1855. Then there were over a hundred fishing-boats working from here. Now there are but a handful.

Up to about 1920 the harbour was also busy with all kind of cargoes, but the railways finished this trade.

In the low huts on the inner breakwater, fish is smoke-cured. Mention you are Footpath-Touring, and John Bird will tell you about his skills. Porthleven has a reputation, too, for producing canned Cornish sea foods and soups.

Two famous pilots of the Second World War were associated with the town. Dambuster Guy Gibson, VC, spent his childhood here. Legless pilot Douglas Bader came here for his honeymoon.

Leave harbour by the Bickford-Smith Institute with its clock-tower, and proceed along the coast road that runs above Porthleven Sands.

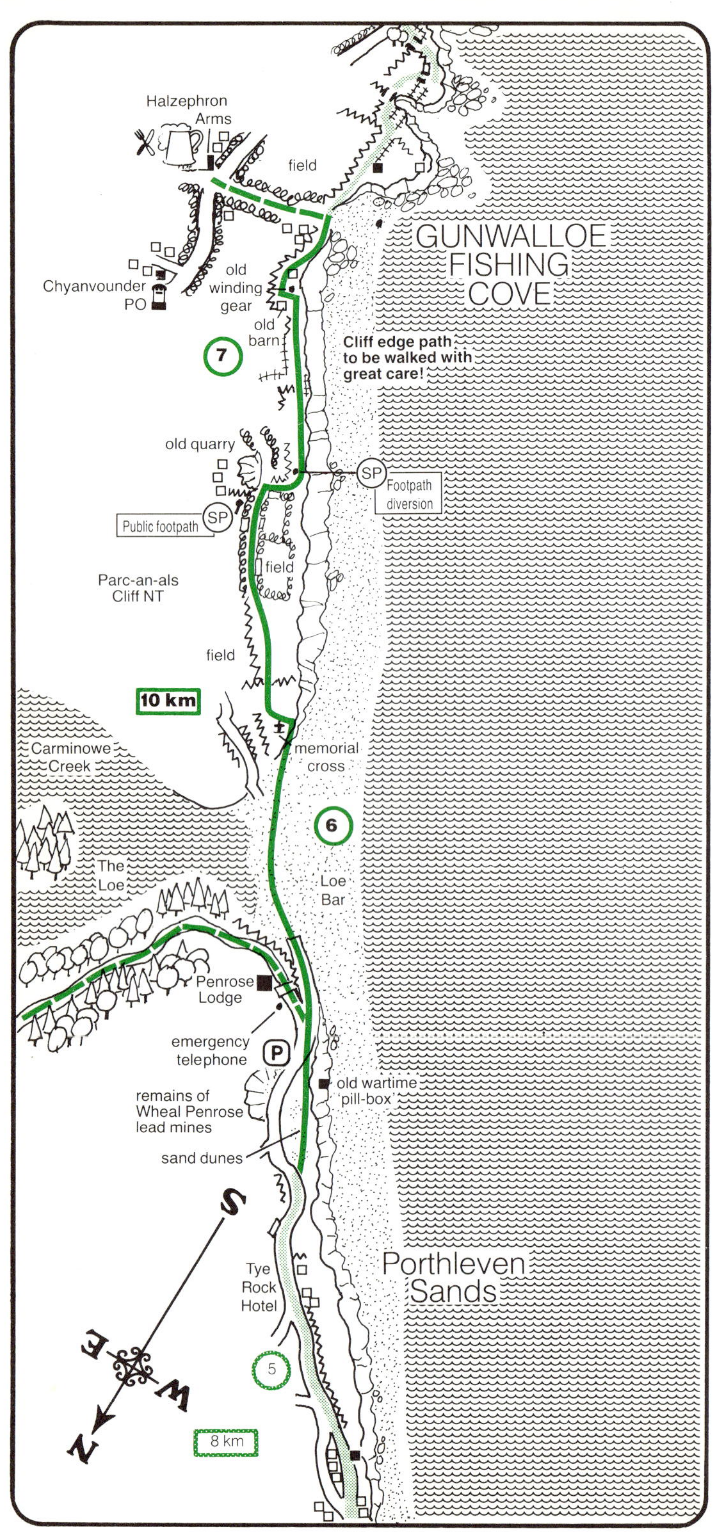
Halzephron
Arms
field
GUNWALLOE
FISHING
COVE
Chyanvounder
PO
old
winding
gear
old
barn
7
Cliff edge path
to be walked with
great care!
old quarry
SP
Footpath
diversion
Public footpath
SP
field
Parc-an-als
Cliff NT
field
10 km
Carminowe
Creek
memorial
cross
6
The
Loe
Loe
Bar
Penrose
Lodge
emergency
telephone
P
old wartime
'pill-box'
remains of
Wheal Penrose
lead mines
sand dunes
S
Tye
Rock
Hotel
Porthleven
Sands
E
W
N
5
8 km

Porthleven Sands to Gunwalloe Fishing Cove

Going: Easy road walk followed by sand dunes, and beach at Loe Bar. Route leaves beach for slightly inland lane, returning to cliffs at Gunwalloe Fishing Cove.

Follow road above beach. A short cut is possible across sand dunes.

On the left of the road can be seen remains of the old Wheal Penrose and Wheal Rose mines, where the prize was not copper or tin, but lead. Tradition says these mines were worked by the Romans. Work stopped in 1844 when the workings were 750 feet *230 m* deep.

At entrance to the Penrose estate (NT), drop down on to Loe Bar beach.

The estate includes the largest lake in Cornwall, the Loe Pool. Legend claims that this was the pool into which the dying King Arthur instructed Sir Bedivere to cast his magical sword Excalibur. It is also claimed that a Spanish treasure-ship was driven over the bar by a storm and still lies deep down in the pool. A pleasant walk round the pool, through bluebells, rare plants, and exotic trees, is freely open to the public from dawn to dusk every day.

The Loe Bar, which dams Loe Pool from the sea, is composed of chalk flint shingle, found only here in all Cornwall. There are large patches of the blue-grey leaves of sea holly, with its attractive blue flowers.

Cross the bar and head for the white cross on the dunes.

This cross marks the wreck of the 44-gun frigate HMS *Anson* which was wrecked on this shore during a violent storm on 28 December 1807. Crowds gathered on the beach and watched horrified and helpless, as a mere stone's throw away, it was pounded to pieces and 120 lives were lost. Those bodies recovered were buried on this cliff. One of the anguished spectators was Henry Trengrouse of Helston who determined to do something to prevent such tragic affairs. He spent his life savings of £3500 and devoted his life to developing a rocket device which could throw a lifeline to a wreck. A grateful Government made him a grant of £50; he is said to have received a diamond ring from the Tsar of Russia; and Helston raised a memorial stone to his memory when he died bankrupt in 1834.

From the cross go diagonally Left to follow a wall that runs behind the dunes. Note: An alternative path runs straight ahead along the cliff edge, but this route allows no margin of error and on no account should be taken in high winds.

Enter hedged lane between fields. At quarry on Left, take track Right down to cliff, and follow cliff path to Gunwalloe Fishing Cove.

The beach here is composed of small pebbles, very suitable for making concrete, and a small concrete-block-making business operates.

Three minutes up the hedged lane to the Left is Chyanvounder hamlet with a very good pub, the Halzephron Arms, a Post Office and telephone.

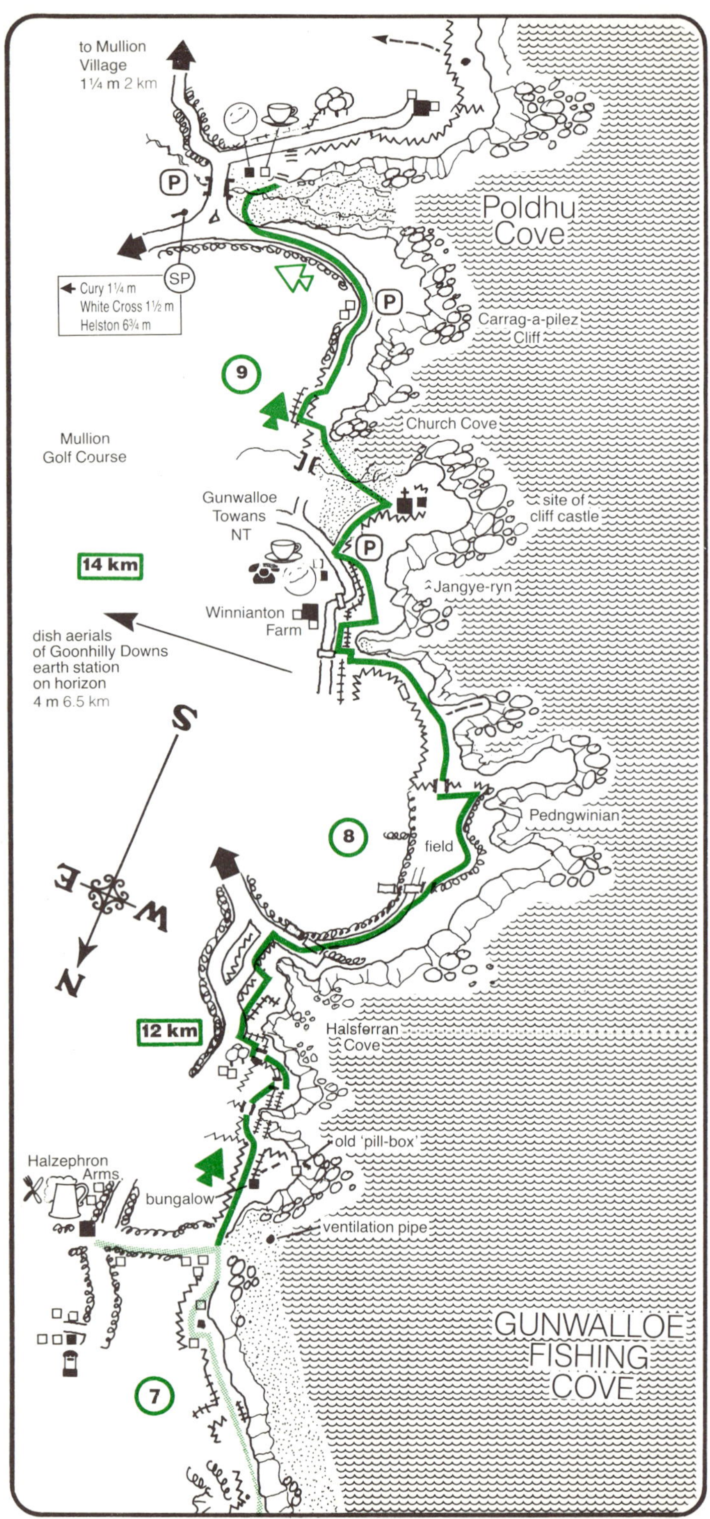

to Mullion
Village
1¼ m 2 km
P
SP
← Cury 1¼ m
White Cross 1½ m
Helston 6¾ m
Poldhu
Cove
P
Carrag-a-pilez
Cliff
9
Church Cove
Mullion
Golf Course
Gunwalloe
Towans
NT
site of
cliff castle
P
14 km
Jangye-ryn
Winnianton
Farm
dish aerials
of Goonhilly Downs
earth station
on horizon
4 m 6.5 km
S
E
W
N
8
field
Pedngwinian
12 km
Halsferran
Cove
old 'pill-box'
Halzephron
Arms
bungalow
ventilation pipe
GUNWALLOE
FISHING
COVE
7

Gunwalloe Fishing Cove to Poldhu Cove

Going: An easy walk along a battered but most attractive stretch of coast.

Leave Gunwalloe Fishing Cove by cliff path, behind bungalow which has been ten years rebuilding.

Fast-disappearing cliffs here result in the path being continually pushed back. However, Cornwall County Council do a good job, keeping the path safe, with the route well indicated and fenced.

At Halsferran Cove, where route briefly joins the road, see how the macadamised highway has been resited three times! Follow signs to walk round edge of field at Pedngwinian. Climb over stone stile to rejoin cliff-edge path, and briefly join farm road at Winniaton.

There is a little detour Right, on to the cliffs at Jangye-ryn, then turn back Left to the road, by toilets and seasonal refreshment hut.

Jangye-ryn is also known locally as Dollar Cove. In 1787 a Spanish vessel was driven ashore here, and was battered to pieces by wild seas. Legend says it was carrying a cargo of 19 tons of silver dollars. Certainly about 1800, young boys were said to be able to dig up coins by the handful.

Follow by wall on Right to the delightful little Church of St Winwaloe, crouching down on the beach, behind protective rock.

A church is thought to have been founded here by monks from Brittany, in the 6thC. The present building probably dates from the 14thC, while the separate bell-tower is possibly much older.

This church knows both the peace of solitude, and the mighty fury of wild wind and waves. For over a thousand years, people have made their way here in search of comfort and guidance, or to offer praise and thanks. Perhaps you, too, can spare a few moments here. Mullion Cove is only one and a half hours of easy walking away, and this seems as fitting a place as any to reflect on where it is you are going.

(Service at 15.00 hrs every Sunday in summer.)

The beach of Church Cove has another legend of treasure. It is said that in 1526 the King of Portugal's treasure-ship, *St Andrew*, foundered here and is buried with 3 tons of silver. In 1785 a ship carrying 2½ tons of gold is also said to have been wrecked here. Gold doubloons and other gold coins have been found on the beach.

The area was the scene of strange episodes about 1845, when local business men were persuaded to finance schemes to retrieve the treasure, either by building a dam, or by mining below the beach. Investors were left poorer and wiser.

A Blessing of the Sea ceremony takes place here every 1 November, All Saints' Day.

Ascend a wide track to the car park at Carrag-a-pilez. Descend by road to beach of Poldhu Cove.

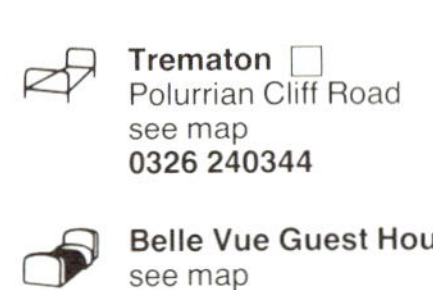

Trematon □
Polurrian Cliff Road
see map
0326 240344

Belle Vue Guest House Ea/S
see map
0326 240483

Henscath House □
see map
0326 240537

Polurrian Hotel A/O
see map
0326 240421

Criggan Mill M/O
see map
0326 240496

see map

in the village

Tonkin's
0326 240137

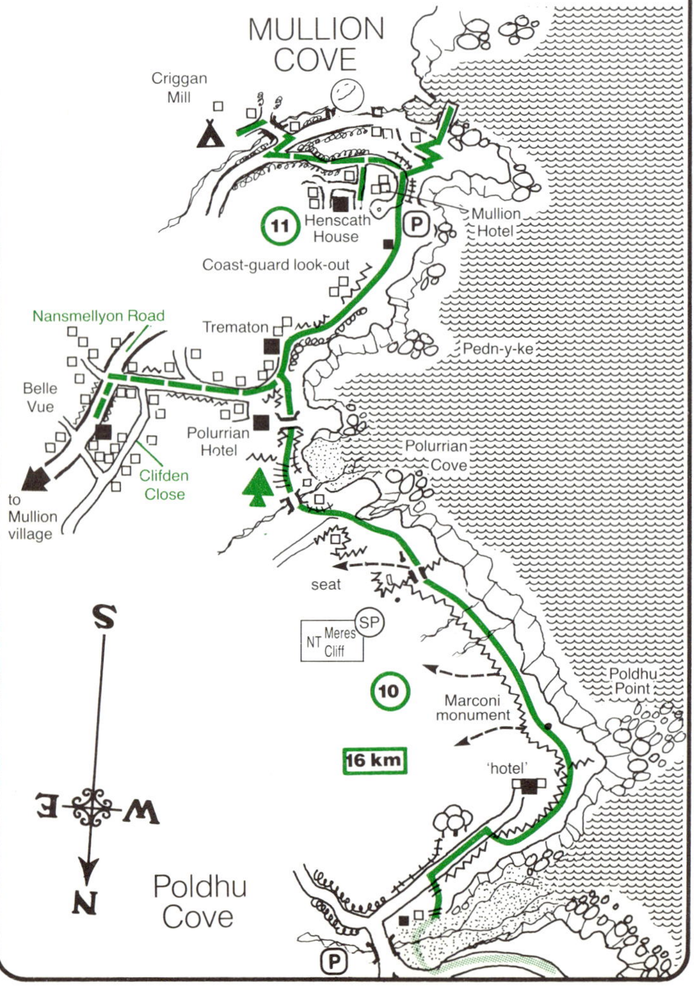

MULLION COVE
Criggan Mill
11
Henscath House
Mullion Hotel
P
Coast-guard look-out
Nansmellyon Road
Trematon
Pedn-y-ke
Belle Vue
Polurrian Hotel
Polurrian Cove
Clifden Close
to Mullion village
seat
NT Meres Cliff
SP
10
Poldhu Point
Marconi monument
16 km
'hotel'
S
W
E
N
Poldhu Cove
P

Poldhu Cove to Mullion Cove

Going: Steep climbs out of Poldhu and Polurrian coves, but otherwise a short, easy, and magnificent cliff-top walk.

Poldhu is said to be Cornish for 'black pool'. This is a popular beach, very busy in the summer. Undertow currents make swimming inadvisable one hour each side of low tide.

Climb up cliff to join road for a few yards, then back on to cliff path to Poldhu Point.

The large building, once an hotel, is now a nursing home.

Follow wall on Left to the prominent pillar of Cornish granite.

This monument recalls the work of Guglielmo Marconi, inventor of wireless. Over the wall can be seen the concrete anchor points, which once supported the four tall steel lattice towers of Marconi's signal station.

In 1901 Marconi began his experiments sending signals without wires. Initially his first efforts were received 225 miles *360 km* away at Crookhaven on the west coast of Ireland. In November Marconi crossed the Atlantic to Newfoundland, 3000 miles *4800 km* away, where on Signal Hill at St John's, he raised a 400 feet *120 m* high kite aerial. On 12 December a jubilant Marconi received the agreed signal, the three 'dots' of the Morse Code letter S, proving that radio waves would follow the curvature of the earth, and world-wide signalling was a possibility.

Four years later a daily news service to all ships was transmitted from the station. The station operated until 1933, and the masts cleared away and a monument erected in 1937.

It is interesting to note that only sixty-one years later, 11 July 1962, the first transatlantic television pictures were received at Goonhilly Downs, just 4 miles *6·5 km* inland from here.

Follow wall on Left, until seat in angled walls on Left, then follow path dropping down towards cliff edge, and walk down to Polurrian Cove.

Stone slabs ease slightly the steep climb up out of the cove. Wicket-gate on Left, just before footbridge over the path, is to Polurrian Hotel.

An original hotel here was completely gutted in a fearsome fire in May 1909. The present three star hotel is not cheap but is much recommended, not least for unmatched views of spectacular sunsets.

Follow cliff road and path round to hotel at Mullion Cove. There are several paths that may be taken down to the harbour. Best is most seaward, which drops down to main breakwater.

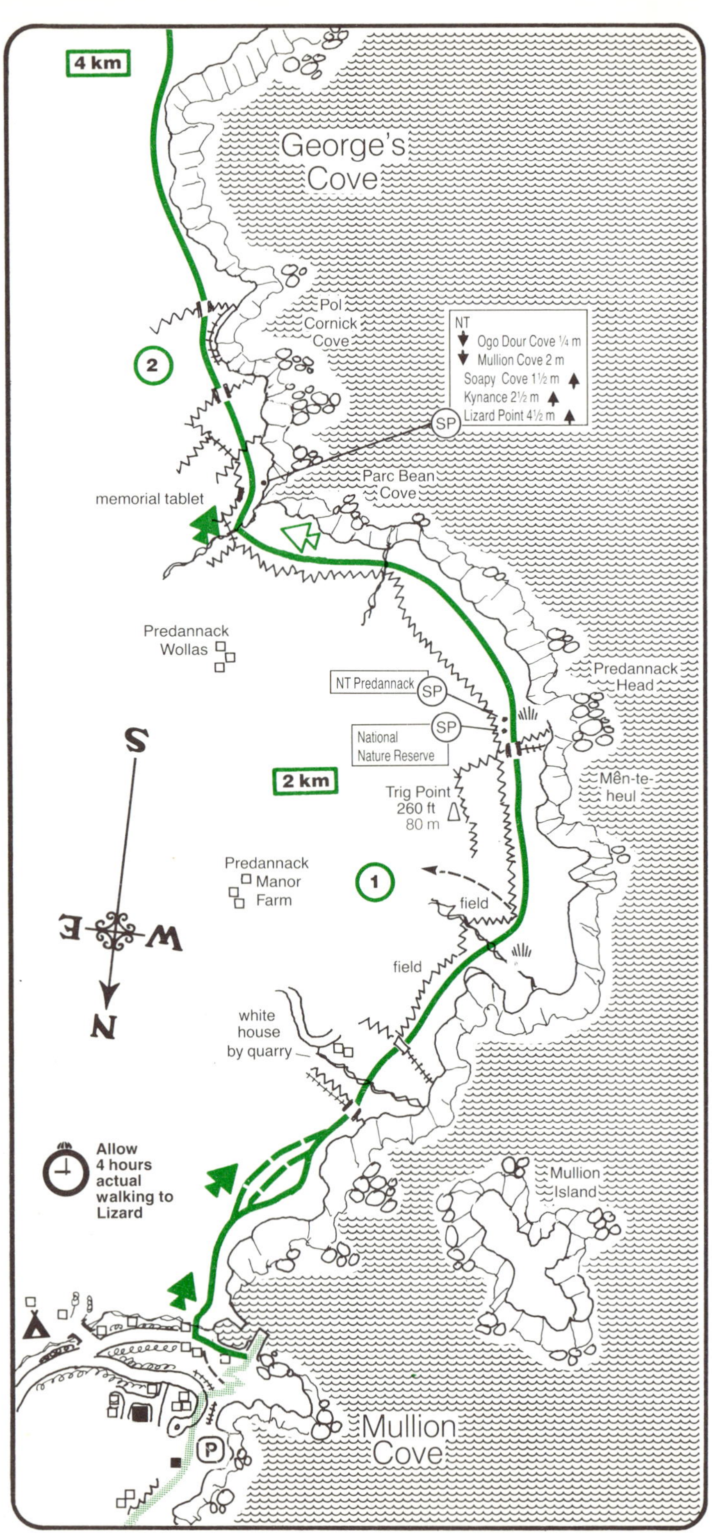
4 km
George's Cove
Pol Cornick Cove
NT
Ogo Dour Cove ¼ m
Mullion Cove 2 m
Soapy Cove 1½ m
Kynance 2½ m
Lizard Point 4½ m
SP
2
Parc Bean Cove
memorial tablet
Predannack Wollas
NT Predannack
SP
Predannack Head
National Nature Reserve
S
2 km
Trig Point 260 ft 80 m
Mên-te-heul
Predannack Manor Farm
1
field
W
E
field
N
white house by quarry
Allow 4 hours actual walking to Lizard
Mullion Island
Mullion Cove
P

Lunch: Kynance Cove is an attractive place for a lunch stop. A refreshment hut down on the beach is open during the height of the season. At the top of the cliffs, by the National Trust car park, is a further refreshment place which is open every day from Easter to the end of October.

Mullion Cove to George's Cove

Going: A steep climb out of the cove is followed by an easy, well-defined cliff walk.

The attractive, much-photographed Mullion Cove was acquired by the National Trust in 1945. The old name was Porth Mellin, Cornish for 'mill cove'.

The harbour was built in 1895 of the very hard, local greenstone. Previously the fishing-boats had stood offshore, and in a terrible storm in 1839 most of the cove's fishing fleet was destroyed.

Two famous Cornish smugglers, Bobo George and John Munday used Mullion Cove as their base, and stored contraband in nearby Torchlight Cave.

From here the rock changes to serpentine for which the Lizard is famous. Local craftsmen produce souvenirs from the blue, grey, and green stone.

Climb any of the many tracks from the cove; those nearest the sea, as always, being most rewarding.

Just offshore, Mullion Island is a bird sanctuary and is closed to the public.

Just beyond a white house, a wall is joined on Left to Predannack Point.

Just beyond the wall is the white pillar of a 'trig' point. In good visibility you should be able to see the coastline you have walked, right back to Hella Point by Porthgwarra (page 19), 23 miles *37 km* across Mounts Bay. If the sun is shining you may even be able to pick out Tater-du automatic lighthouse, white against the foot of cliffs, 15 miles *24 km* away.

These cliffs, together with Mullion Cliffs, form the Lizard Nature Reserve, one of the most important heathland sites in Britain. The area contains many rare heathers, grasses, and plants, some of which are unique to these cliffs. All but three of Britain's twenty native clovers are to be found here. The reserve is under the protection of the Nature Conservancy Council from which free leaflets are available (see inside back cover).

The path drops down to cross stream at Parc Bean Cove, and climbs up to join wall by memorial tablet.

The memorial records the presentation of this land to the National Trust in memory of the Collins family of Cornwall.

Continue along cliff-top path to George's Cove.

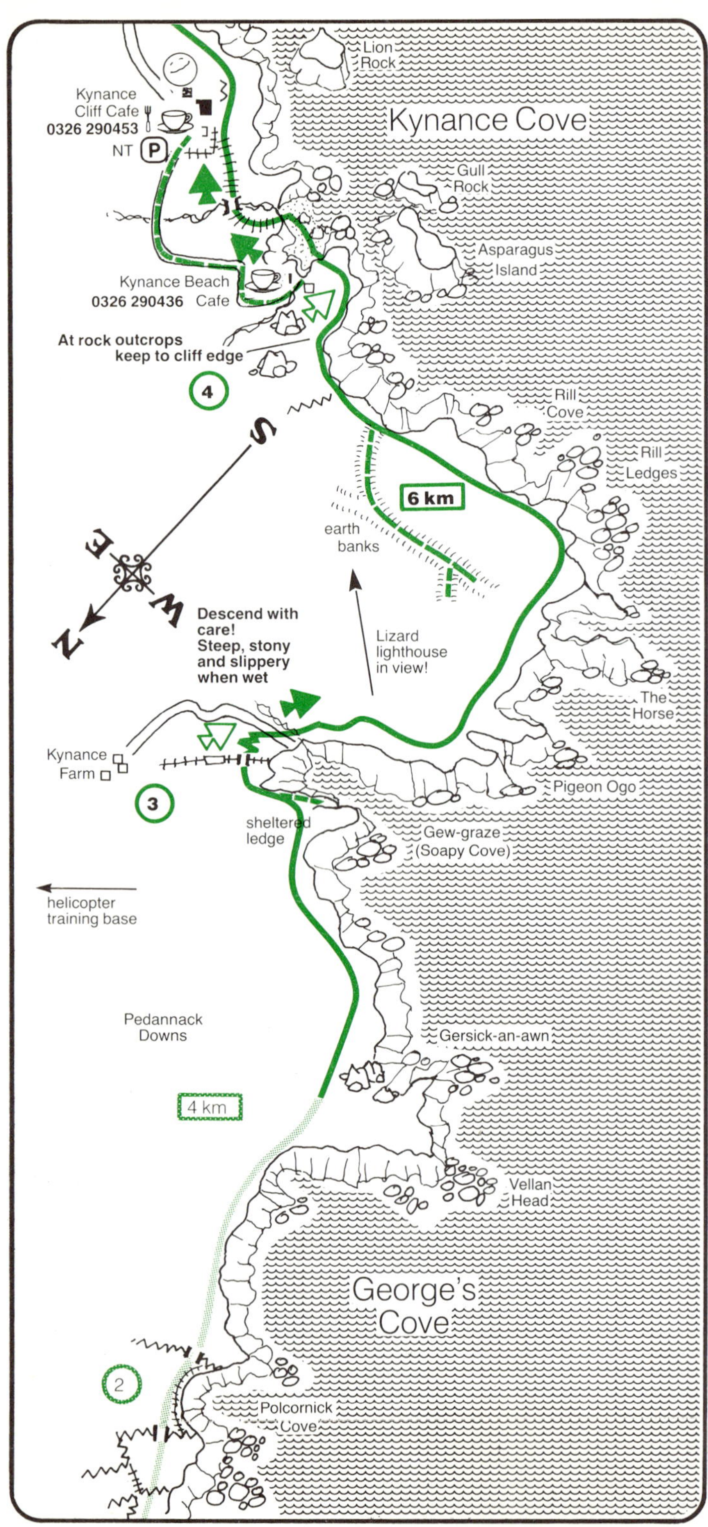
Lion Rock
Kynance Cove
Kynance Cliff Cafe
0326 290453
NT
P
Gull Rock
Asparagus Island
Kynance Beach Cafe
0326 290436
At rock outcrops keep to cliff edge
4
S
Rill Cove
Rill Ledges
6 km
earth banks
E
W
N
Descend with care!
Steep, stony and slippery when wet
Lizard lighthouse in view!
The Horse
Kynance Farm
3
Pigeon Ogo
sheltered ledge
Gew-graze (Soapy Cove)
helicopter training base
Pedannack Downs
Gersick-an-awn
4 km
Vellan Head
George's Cove
2
Polcornick Cove

George's Cove to Kynance Cove

Going: Another magnificent cliff walk, although it can be a bit bleak if the weather is unkind. One steep up-and-down at Gew-Graze.

From the cliff-edge path at George's Cove, the route tends to go straight ahead now, rather than follow the cliffs to the Right, out to Vellam Head. However if time and legs are willing, the cliff route is the most attractive.

On most days throughout the year you are likely to be buzzed by friendly helicopters. These are from the Royal Naval Helicopter School on the Predannack Airfield half a mile inland. The helicopters often come close enough for you to see clearly the pilots, and a friendly wave may be called for. However, don't expect a reply. He is probably bathed in sweat and wondering why he didn't get a job in local government!

Predannack was an important and busy airfield for both fighters and bombers during the Second World War.

Alongside one of the main runways still stands the railway and ramp built in 1950 by Dr Barnes Wallis, inventor of the Dambusters' bomb, when he was here conducting trials on swing-wing aircraft.

Predannack Airfield is now part of HMS *Seahawk*, the Royal Naval Air Station at Culdrose, the largest naval air station and helicopter base in Europe. The Navy also operates its superb 24-hour, 365-day air-sea rescue service from here, and the familiar giant yellow helicopters 'chopping' along, just above the cliffs, are a heart-warming and welcome sight.

The 'ahead' path rejoins the cliffs at the steep-sided cove of Gew-Graze.

There is a sheltered ledge here, facing south, which makes a blissful coffee stop.

Steep path down to cross stream needs to be negotiated with care, particularly when wet.

The quarry workings in Gew-Graze mark where, in 1755, Richard Chaffers of Liverpool, discovered soapstone (steatite), which enabled him to produce high-quality porcelain, which was said to be the envy of the great Josiah Wedgwood. Chaffers later founded the Worcester Porcelain Company.

Climb steeply up out of cove. A detour of a few steps can be made to dramatic Pigeon Ogo.

The vertical, craggy rock faces a 200 feet *60 m* drop down to an often furious sea, while every crag and ledge is sometimes crowded with screeching sea-birds.

Follow the cliffs vaguely round by any route to Rill Cove.

Here tradition has it that the Spanish Armada of 1588 was first sighted as it sailed into the English Channel, causing warning bonfires to be lit throughout the land.
In the distance you can see a low white building with six black chimneys, between two white stubby towers. This is Lizard Lighthouse!

A rough path leads round and down to the scenic and famous Kynance Cove. A sheltered and delightful lunch stop.

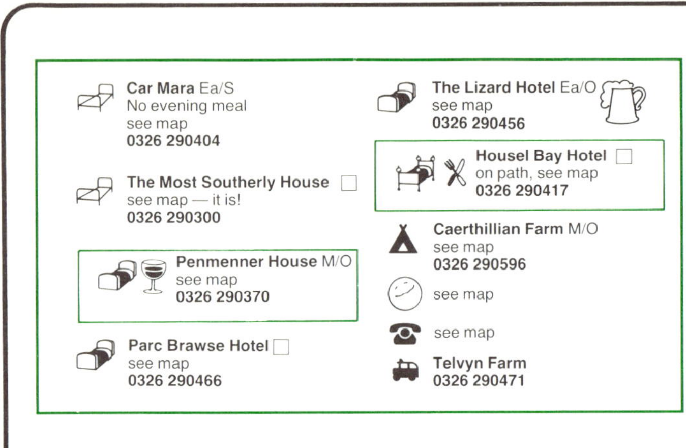
Car Mara Ea/S
No evening meal
see map
0326 290404

The Most Southerly House ☐
see map — it is!
0326 290300

Penmenner House M/O
see map
0326 290370

Parc Brawse Hotel ☐
see map
0326 290466

The Lizard Hotel Ea/O
see map
0326 290456

Housel Bay Hotel ☐
on path, see map
0326 290417

Caerthillian Farm M/O
see map
0326 290596

see map

see map

Telvyn Farm
0326 290471

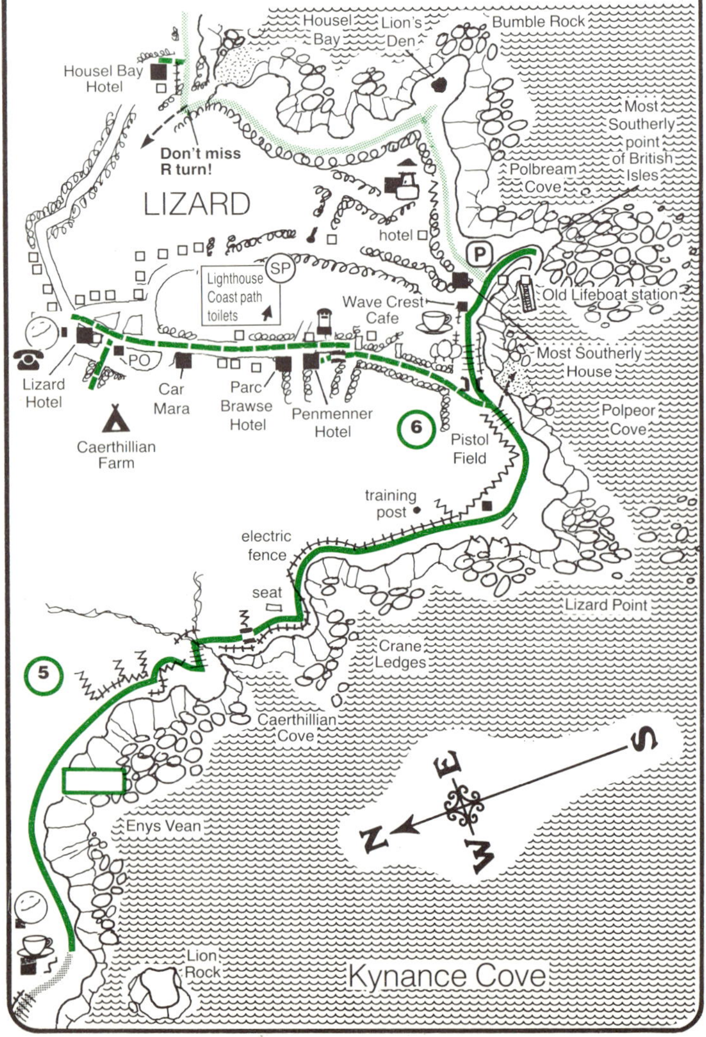

Housel Bay
Lion's Den
Bumble Rock
Housel Bay Hotel
Most Southerly point of British Isles
Don't miss R turn!
Polbream Cove
LIZARD
hotel
P
SP
Lighthouse
Coast path
toilets
Old Lifeboat station
Wave Crest Cafe
Most Southerly House
PO
Lizard Hotel
Car Mara
Parc Brawse Hotel
Penmenner Hotel
Polpeor Cove
6
Pistol Field
Caerthillian Farm
training post
electric fence
seat
Lizard Point
Crane Ledges
5
Caerthillian Cove
S
E
N
W
Enys Vean
Lion Rock
Kynance Cove

Kynance Cove to The Lizard

Going: A popular and easy walk along spectacular cliff tops.

Kynance Cove (NT) has excited travellers, artists, and writers for many years. At high tide, the sea rushes and swirls round peaks of serpentine with names like Gull Rock, Steeple Rock, and Sugar Loaf. At low tide, yellow sands give access to these rock islands and splendid caves known as The Drawing Room, and The Parlour.

The largest island is Asparagus Rock, so called because of the wild asparagus that grows there. At the base of this rock, at certain states of the tide, a low booming noise and a shower of spray emanates from a blow-hole known locally as The Devil's Bellows.

At low tide, the route passes across the beach and climbs 200 feet *60 m*, by steep steps, to the cliff refreshment place and car park. (To learn state of the tide, see page 15.)

The 109 granite steps were once paving setts in the town of Helston.

At high tide it will be necessary to turn Left by the *beach* refreshment hut, and follow the drive round to the Right, to achieve the car park.

Follow the well-pounded route which wanders along the wild cliff top.

Signs of serpentine quarrying are evident each side of the path.

A Coastguard look-out hut marks Lizard Point. Although often quoted as the most southerly point of the British Isles, this distinction in fact belongs to Polpeor Cove, ½ mile *1 km* farther along the path.

The rocks that reach seaward for ½ mile *1 km* have been the scourge of shipping throughout the ages, and are still distrusted by today's mariners.

One of the larger rocks is known as the Man-of-War. It is said to get this name from the wreck of the man-o'-war *Royal Anne* in 1721. The ship was smashed against the rock and reduced to splinters. Only 3 survived from a crew of 200. The bodies that were washed ashore were buried in Pistol Field.

At the low-lying Pistol Field a decision must be made. If you just wish to get to Lizard village, to fall into that hot bath, and prepare for dinner, then take the footpath to the Left that follows a stream. This leads to a hedged lane taking you directly up into Lizard. If you desire to stand on Britain's most southerly point, treat yourself to a cup of tea or ice cream, buy a serpentine souvenir, or gaze at the visitors, then climb steps ahead.

Note: The passage of cars along the narrow, high-banked road from Polpeor to Lizard makes walking a dangerous activity. Better to retrace down steps to Pistol Field, and take footpath.

If Lizard marks the end of your Footpath-Touring adventure, congratulations on your perseverance. I hope you enjoyed it. If you propose walking on to Coverack tomorrow morning, sleep well!

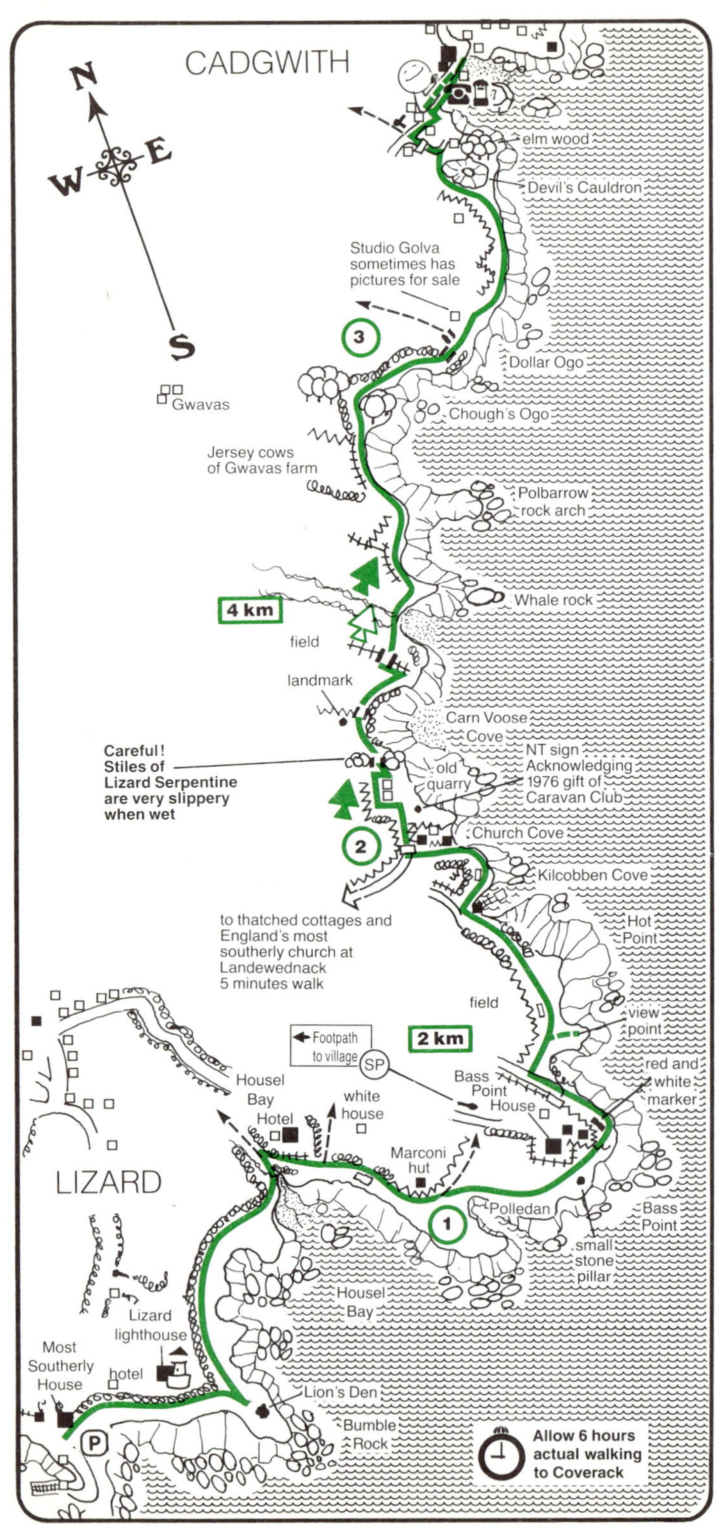
CADGWITH
N
W
E
S
elm wood
Devil's Cauldron
Studio Golva sometimes has pictures for sale
3
Dollar Ogo
Gwavas
Chough's Ogo
Jersey cows of Gwavas farm
Polbarrow rock arch
Whale rock
4 km
field
landmark
Carn Voose Cove
Careful! Stiles of Lizard Serpentine are very slippery when wet
old quarry
NT sign Acknowledging 1976 gift of Caravan Club
Church Cove
2
Kilcobben Cove
to thatched cottages and England's most southerly church at Landewednack 5 minutes walk
Hot Point
field
view point
2 km
Footpath to village
SP
red and white marker
Bass Point House
Housel Bay
Hotel
white house
Marconi hut
LIZARD
Polledan
1
Bass Point
small stone pillar
Housel Bay
Lizard lighthouse
Most Southerly House
hotel
Lion's Den
Bumble Rock
P
Allow 6 hours actual walking to Coverack

Lunch: The inn at Cadgwith provides good snacks, including superb seafood. However it is only two hours' walk from Lizard. You could make a late start, but remember that from Cadgwith to Coverack will take you about four hours' walking. Alternatively carry a packed lunch for a picnic on Kennack Sands.

Lizard to Cadgwith

Going: A fascinating path that mostly keeps to the edge of cliffs.

From Polpeor Cove, cliff path passes in front of Polbream Hotel and Lighthouse. Open to public Monday to Friday from 12.00 hrs.

There has been a lighthouse here since 1619. Present building dates from 1751. Originally, the light came from coal fires in both towers. Now the single lamp can be seen for 21 miles *34 km* and the double boom of the splendid fog-horns can be heard 14 miles *22 km* away.

A short detour leads to Lion's Den. Examine with care!

A narrow cliff-edge path leads down to Housel Cove, with low-tide beach. Turn to Right to pass in front of Housel Bay Hotel.

When the *QE2* passed the Lizard on her way home from the Falklands campaign, carrying 700 survivors, Thomas Stanley, owner of the hotel and a Navy man, made a signal with the Aldis lamp he keeps by the bar. 'Well done. Welcome home. God bless.'

Continue along cliff path to the cleft of Polledan. The wooden hut was used by Marconi in transmission experiments to the Isle of Wight 176 miles *280 km* away.

Follow path round cliff edge to white Bass Point House.

This was a Lloyd's signal station up to December 1969.

The path passes beneath obsolete and current Coastguard look-out posts. Vertical red and white stripes on a wall are explained when you look back to Bass Point House. Matching stripes provide markers similar to cones on Hella Point (page 19).

See Coastguard's look-out on Black Head, 4½ miles *7 km* across bay.

Path descends into Kilcobben Cove with its lifeboat station, opened in 1961 to replace the stations of Lizard and Cadgwith. You can usually inspect the 52 foot *16 m* lifeboat *Duke of Cornwall* if you can face returning up those steep and daunting steps. (The lift is for crew only!)

Follow path round to Church Cove, a lifeboat station in 1885 but soon abandoned due to difficulty in launching.

Turn Right along lane behind old quarries. Climb up to cliff-edge path, beneath white diamond navigation landmark. Looking back, among trees, are the four pinnacles of England's most southerly church, St. Winwaloe, Landewednack.

Beyond Carn Voose Cove, a narrow path squeezes along between green fields and steep cliff edges to the rim of the spectacular collapsed cave of Hugga Driggee.

When east winds blow, and the tide is high, boiling seas and thrashing pebbles earn the popular name of Devil's Cauldron. Here is a small wood of Dwarf Elm, unique in Britain.

Past cottages the route turns Right, to drop down through attractive private gardens, to join road down into Cadgwith.

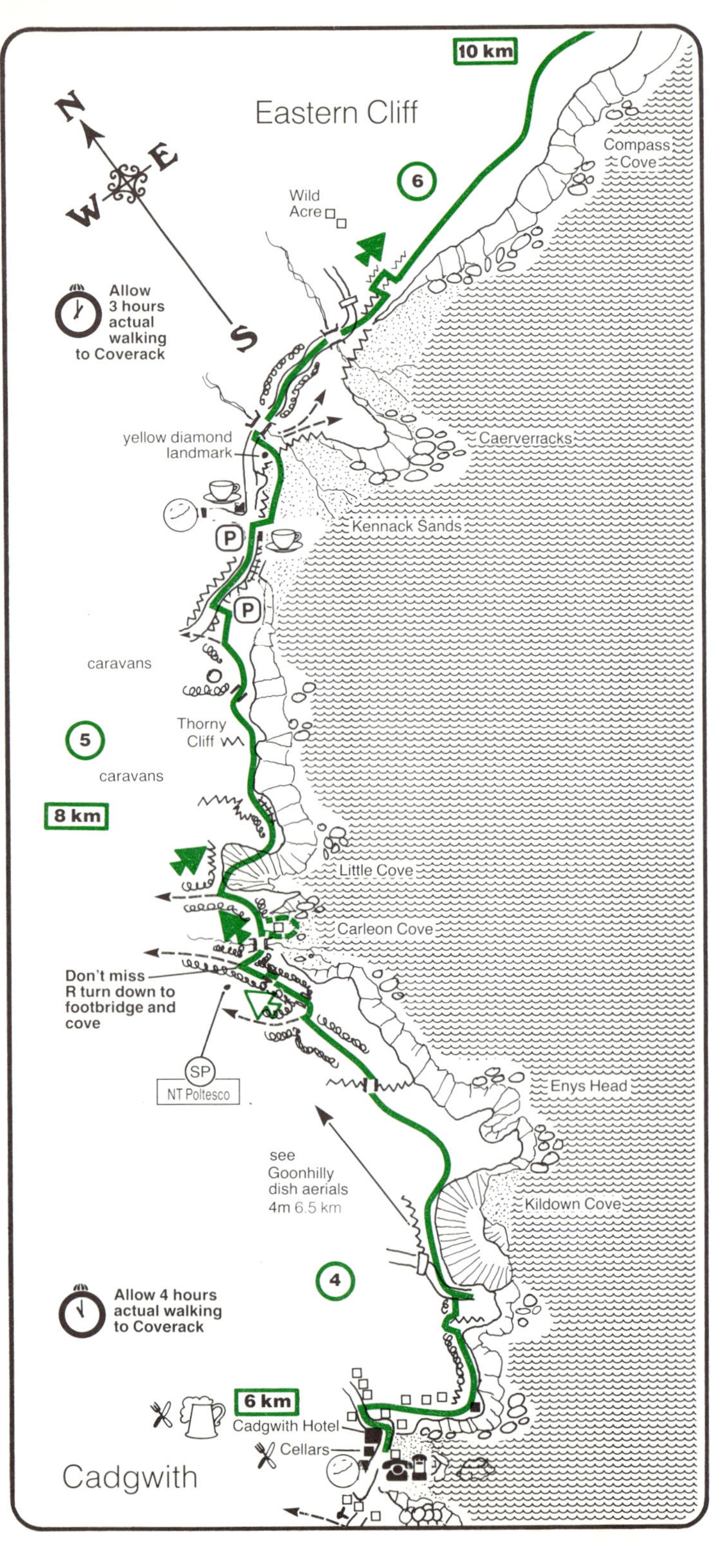
10 km
Eastern Cliff
N
E
W
S
Compass Cove
6
Wild Acre
Allow 3 hours actual walking to Coverack
Caerverracks
yellow diamond landmark
Kennack Sands
P
P
caravans
Thorny Cliff
5
caravans
8 km
Little Cove
Carleon Cove
Don't miss R turn down to footbridge and cove
SP
NT Poltesco
Enys Head
see Goonhilly dish aerials 4m 6.5 km
Kildown Cove
4
Allow 4 hours actual walking to Coverack
6 km
Cadgwith Hotel
Cellars
Cadgwith

Cadgwith to Eastern Cliff

Going: An easy walk with some ups and downs, and a pleasant stretch along a popular beach.

Cadgwith is an attractive fishing village. This was one of the many villages that thrived on the pilchard trade. Enormous catches were often made. These were stacked in salt in the cellars in high piles, for four to five weeks. The weight forced the oil out into channels, and this was collected and sold for various commercial uses including soap-making and leather-dressing. The fish were then packed into barrels and shipped abroad where they were much in demand. The pilchard cellars, or 'palaces', still stand at Cadgwith.

In 1867 a lifeboat station was established here with a boat that bore the splendid name of *The Western Commercial Traveller*. A new boat presented by the Girl Guides of Britain in 1940 was dispatched instantly to the evacuation beaches of Dunkirk, and was last launched in 1963. A list of the achievements of the station can be seen at the entrance to the Old Cellars Restaurant.

The pleasant thatched cottages have housed famous people, including the distinguished pianist Dame Myra Hess, and the artist David Shepherd, painter of elephants, tigers, and trains. His portrait of a late local fisherman hangs in the bar of the excellent inn.

Leave Cadgwith by the road that leads up past the inn, and turn Right up a narrow lane towards the cliffs.

On the cliff edge stands a huer's hut, restored by the National Trust.

It was the huer's job to watch for the shoals of pilchards. When a shoal was espied he would raise a 'hue' to call out all the available fishermen. From his vantage point on the cliffs he would direct where the nets should be dropped by using 'bats', forerunner of those used today on aircraft-carriers.

The path passes behind Kildown Cove and enters a hedged lane to drop down to Carelon Cove. Don't miss the Right turn to cross the footbridge.

This beach was once the site of a busy factory, producing serpentine mantelpieces and shop-fronts still to be found in London and Paris. Queen Victoria ordered a table to be specially made. The enterprise closed in 1889, but now the owners, the National Trust, are restoring the buildings, perhaps to install a serpentine museum. The initials to be found on the building stand for Lizard Serpentine Company.

Beyond Little Cove the path follows the cliff edge, skirting a large caravan park. At a cliff car park, turn Right on to the road running down to Kennack Sands.

The yellow diamond sign marks where a cable was laid in 1971 to Bilbao, northern Spain.

If it is high tide, take the lane that leaves behind the concrete breakwater, to cross behind the serpentine headland of Caerverracks. If tide is well out, you may walk the beach.

At the end of the far beach take the path that begins at the end of breakwater, to climb a thin track steeply up Eastern Cliff.

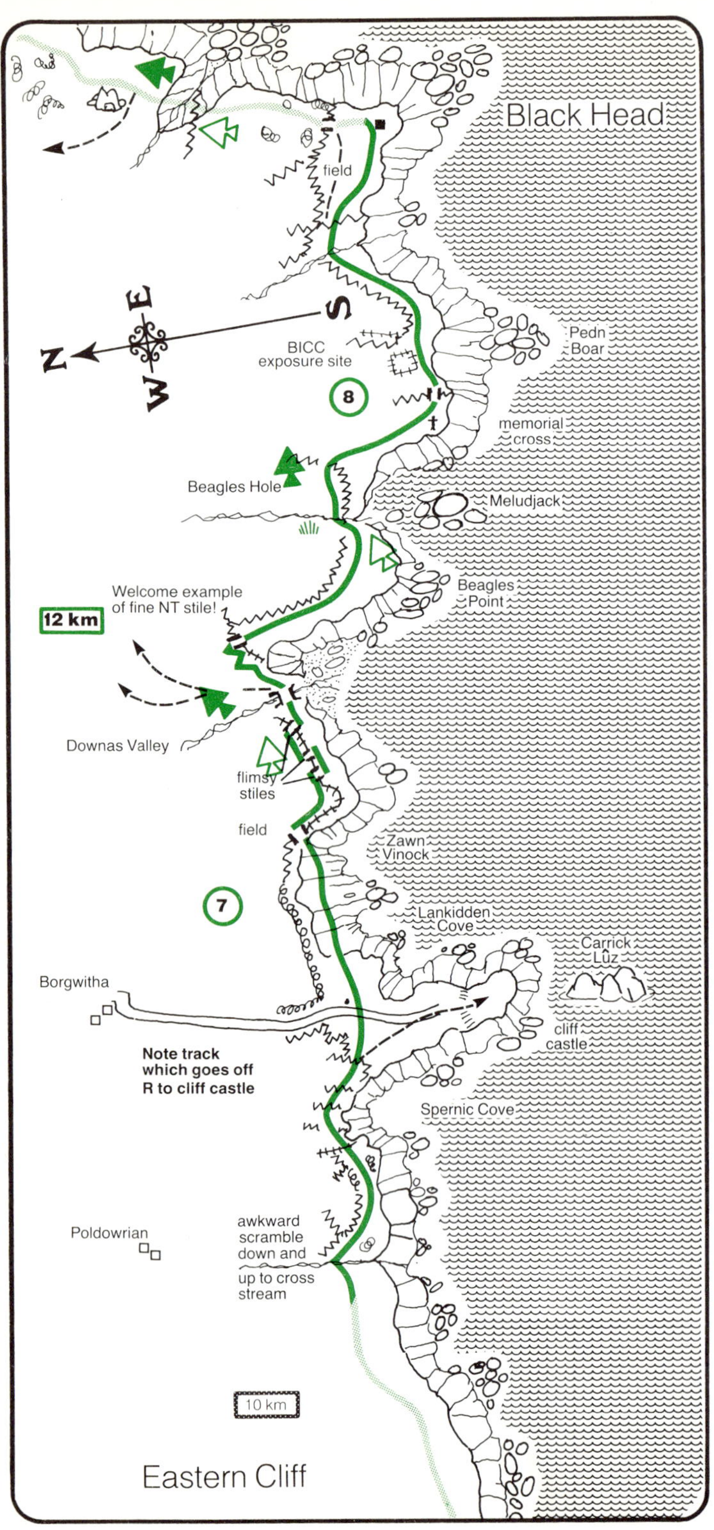
Black Head
field
S
E
N
W
BICC
exposure site
Pedn
Boar
8
memorial
cross
Beagles Hole
Meludjack
Beagles
Point
Welcome example
of fine NT stile!
12 km
Downas Valley
flimsy
stiles
field
Zawn
Vinock
7
Lankidden
Cove
Carrick
Lûz
Borgwitha
cliff
castle
Note track
which goes off
R to cliff castle
Spernic Cove
Poldowrian
awkward
scramble
down and
up to cross
stream
10 km
Eastern Cliff

Eastern Cliff to Black Head

Going: Not a frequently walked path, so sometimes requires care in selecting right track, especially behind headland of Carrick Lûz. A steep up-and-down at Downas Cove, followed by a less dramatic dip at Beagles Hole makes this section fairly strenuous. But fine coastal walking all the way.

Follow narrow cliff-top track through heather and bracken.

Where there is a choice of tracks, follow the simple rule of not wandering too far from the sea on your Right!

There is an awkward scramble to cross a stream below Poldowrian Farm. Care is also required to avoid following a field track which goes diagonally off to Right, to the cliff castle at Carrick Lûz. (Unless of course you wish to detour to visit this historic site and fine viewpoint.) Carrick Lûz is Cornish for 'great grey rock'. Correct path goes ahead to follow wall on Left, to cross the Borgwitha/Carrick Lûz Farm track. A small stone marker indicates where indistinct path leaves farm track, across very rough terrain, behind Lankidden Cove. Climb prominent stile into field and follow cliff-edge fence on Right, down into Downas Cove.

At time of writing the stiles down into Downas are disgusting. But take heart, from here on stiles are new and beautifully built. (Thank you once again National Trust.)

Cross stream and take the track nearest to the sea up the steep flank of Downas. Adopt a steady pace at the bottom, and you will do the climb easily!

At top, cross good stile to follow cliff-edge path, with wall on your Left, to the often boggy depression at Beagles Point. Through wall at top and follow clear cliff-top track, past small memorial cross, to high fenced enclosure at Pedn Boar.

The high wire fence marks the exposure site where BICC General Cables subject coatings and colours to sea-air life tests.

Follow wall on Left, then cliff edge, to reach the Coastguard hut on Black Head.

Incidentally, those two cliff-top pulleys back by Folly Cove (page 19), are relics of a wartime tank training ground. A tank silhouette was towed back and forth on a cable round the pulleys. The shells went out to sea! I expect you guessed.

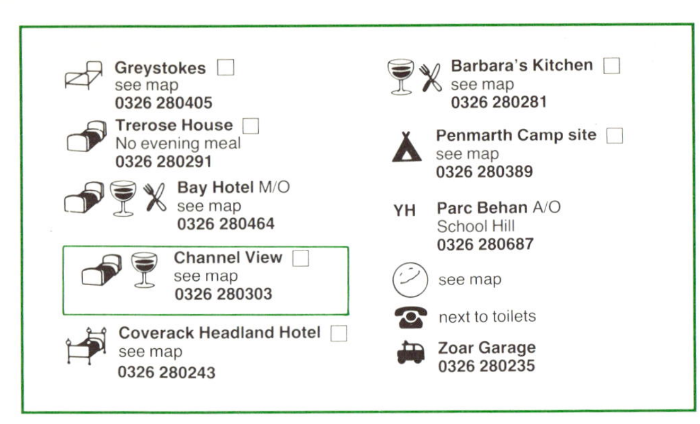
Greystokes
see map
0326 280405
Trerose House
No evening meal
0326 280291
Bay Hotel M/O
see map
0326 280464
Channel View
see map
0326 280303
Coverack Headland Hotel
see map
0326 280243
Barbara's Kitchen
see map
0326 280281
Penmarth Camp site
see map
0326 280389
YH
Parc Behan A/O
School Hill
0326 280687
see map
next to toilets
Zoar Garage
0326 280235

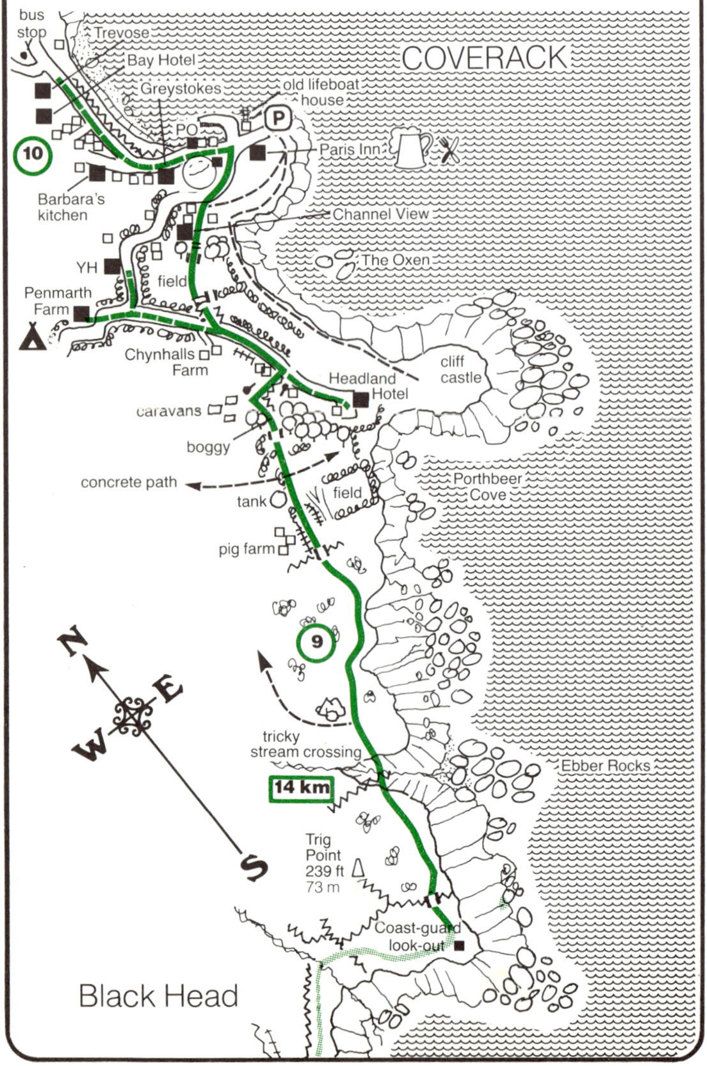

bus stop
Trevose
Bay Hotel
Greystokes
old lifeboat house
P
COVERACK
PO
Paris Inn
10
Barbara's kitchen
Channel View
YH
field
The Oxen
Penmarth Farm
Chynhalls Farm
cliff castle
Headland Hotel
caravans
boggy
concrete path
tank
field
Porthbeer Cove
pig farm
9
N
E
W
S
tricky stream crossing
Ebber Rocks
14 km
Trig Point
239 ft
73 m
Coast-guard look-out
Black Head

Black Head to Coverack

Going: A long, twisting, but well-maintained path through heathland along Chynhalls Cliff. For a brief tortuous stretch, the route loses sight of sea, but then suddenly the path drops rapidly into Coverack.

Past Black Head Coastguard look-out, cross stone wall from grass field on to cliff-top heathland. A twisting, turning path, hacked out of heather, gorse, and bracken, provides dramatic views of rocks and sea below.

Ahead is the very prominent Headland Hotel with the cliff castle of Chynhalls Point beyond. In the distance, beyond Coverack, lies Lowland Point, which rose to put the cliffs 200 feet *60 m* inland when relieved of the pressure of ice at the end of the Ice Age.

The path now passes a richly pungent pig farm. The jungle-like terrain, and loss of the sea should cause you no concern, just press ahead. Suddenly there are caravans on your Left, and a sharp Right turn brings you out to houses and the Headland Hotel road. Turn Left on the road.

Opposite Chynhalls Farm leave road into walled lane on Right. Follow track diagonally Right across a field which drops down to the sea. In trees, enter the welcoming lane and houses of Coverack.

Coverack, once known as Porth Coverac, was another village where the fishermen depended upon the pilchard. On the harbour still stands the old cellars (The Salt Cellar). The small harbour, with its squat sea-wall still houses fishing-boats, but the majority of the craft are for pleasure only.

The village also has a reputation for being deeply involved in once-thriving smuggling activities. Anywhere along this coast has its own legends about the 'free-traders' and their constant tussle with the Revenue men.

A Coverack story tells how John Carlyon, a very active local smuggler, was often saved from discovery by his wife, who would hang a large red shirt on her washing-line whenever it was unsafe for him to come ashore.

Every August, the local choirs and a brass band assemble on the harbour to sing hymns. The service is often included by the BBC in their television 'Songs of Praise' series.

The Paris Inn on the harbour gets its name from the 10 000 ton American liner which ran aground in fog off Lowland Point in May 1899. The 750 passengers were all taken off by Falmouth and Porthoustock lifeboat, and the ship refloated six weeks later.

That's it. You have finished this coastal Footpath-Touring route. Well done!

South West Peninsula Coastal Path

This Footpath-Touring route is very largely along the long-distance footpath that wanders for 563 miles *904 km* round England's south-west peninsula, from Minehead in Somerset to Bournemouth in Poole Bay, Dorset.

It is a magnificent path, full of variety and interest. The walking includes splendid cliffs, long beaches, hidden coves, busy seaside resorts, and picturesque fishing villages. And always the sea, in all its moods, is never far away.

I have a great affection for every bit of this long walk, but in my opinion, this section from Pendeen to the Lizard, the sole of the foot of England, offers the most spectacular coastal walking in England.

Mining in Cornwall: Cornwall has been associated with metals for as long as there has been history. Popular legend claims that Phoenician traders, from the coast of ancient Syria bartered for tin on Porthcurno beach. Both tin and copper were traded with Ireland and the Continent during the Bronze Age (2300–800 BC). Truro Museum has an 150 lb ingot of Cornish tin that probably dates from about 100 BC. The Romans are known to have made use of Cornish tin and copper.

Prior to the Middle Ages the ores were obtained by washing from river deposits, known as 'streaming'.

True 'mining' probably began on the coast where a tin or copper vein, or lode, was exposed in cliffs. A tunnel, or level, or gallery could be driven in to obtain the ore. These tunnels were usually sloped gently up, so that they were self-draining. Cornish miners call these 'adits'. However, quite unlike the horizontal veins of coal, both tin and copper lodes tend to be almost vertical. Working up into the lode presented few problems: these developed when work began to mine the ore below the adit, and water dropped down into the workings rather than run down the sloping tunnel.

Cornish miners became experts at pumping out water by various means, using man-, horse-, and water-power.

Up to the beginning of the 18thC. tin was the main ore searched for, but by the middle of the century the importance of copper became apparent. Then that great launcher, the Industrial Revolution, massively increased demand, and the Cornish mining industry exploded to become the world's largest supplier of copper.

The old water problem now became a major battle, and led to the important part played by Cornish mining in the development of the steam-engine. Steam-power operated the water-pumps, as well as providing lifting power. During this period Cornwall produced first-class mining engineers and scientists, including the great Trevithick and Sir Humphry Davy.

The end of the 19thC. saw the end of the copper boom for Cornwall, with new, cheaper sources opening up in other parts of the world.

However it was discovered that many of the old copper-mines contained deposits of tin, and from about 1869 to 1873 there was a boom in tin. This was cut short by the discovery in Australia of vast alluvial deposits, and Cornwall's industry faltered almost to a halt.

Occasional fluctuations in demand occurred but famous mines disappeared and the mining industry was reduced to the melancholy ruins to be seen on this Footpath-Touring route. Today, Geever is one of the few remaining working tin-mines in all Cornwall.

The Levant Mine disaster: Although the mines made some investors rich, and some landowners richer, for the miner himself the life was very hard. Often his day would begin with a long cliff-top walk to the mine head. Then followed a long climb down vertical ladders, sometimes as much as 1500 feet *500 m*. He would then do a six- or eight-hour shift of hard manual labour in hot, wet conditions, where the only illumination came from a candle poked into a lump of clay, pressed on to his helmet. His lunch was often a meal of potatoes and meat in a pastry case. Because his dirty hands might carry traces of arsenic, he would hold the meal only by the pronounced ridge incorporated in the pastry case, which he would then throw away. (This became the famous Cornish pasty!) After his shift there was the arm and leg agony of the long climb back up vertical ladders, and the walk home.

In an effort to avoid the ladder-climbing, which often produced casualties (and probably meant less efficient miners) the man-engine was invented. A large steam-engine operated an arm which raised and lowered a beam reaching down into the depths of the shaft. This beam had little standing platforms down its length. A miner would leap on to a platform at the top of the beam's 12 foot *4 m* stroke, and then at the bottom of its stroke, would jump off, in the dark, on to a little platform in the wall of the shaft. At the next top of the stroke he would again leap on to the beam, each time being taken 12 feet *4 m* farther down the shaft. The reverse hazardous procedure would bring him to the surface at the end of his shift.

On 20 October 1919, the hinge at the top of the beam snapped, (you can see it in the Geevor Mine Museum), and the 300-fathom beam crumpled down into the shaft, taking its human cargo with it. Thirty-one miners died that day and many were seriously injured.

Down at the Levant Mine you can see the crater that marks the man-engine shaft (see page 8). Across the road is the concrete floor of the old 'dry' where the miners would change from their red, sodden working clothes, and take a bath. The oval trench in the floor is one of the remaining baths where three miners at a time would bathe. A few paces away, now filled by debris, is the entrance to the tunnel that took the miners under the road to the man-engine. On the far edge of the road is the concrete-topped shaft that once illuminated the tunnel. The first indication of the great disaster came when some washing miners realised that men had stopped appearing from the tunnel at the regular rate of one every twelve seconds, and one went to investigate . . .

Cliff-edge towers of Botallack: There has been mining at Botallack since the 1700s and early tales told of miners being afeared of the sea-bed noises just above their heads! The lowest building on the cliff edge is the Crowns pumping engine-house built in 1830 with a shaft going down 800 feet *240 m*. Note the massive blocks of granite used in the building, and consider the problems. The slightly higher building is Pearce's engine-house built about 1860, which operated winding gear for the Boscawen diagonal shaft. This famous shaft ran from the cliffs, 30 feet *9 m* above sea-level, inclined at 32½ degrees, for 2500 feet *760 m*. Royalty were among the VIPs who made a trip down the shaft before it was closed in 1874. As a result of an appeal 110 years later, funds were raised to preserve both engine-houses in 1984.

Zawn Reeth: In 1869 the Telegraph Act set a date when companies in the exciting field of telegraphy were to be taken over by the Government with generous compensation. Small companies rushed to install cables in order to benefit. One company raced against time to lay a submarine cable from Zawn Reeth to the Isles of Scilly. They had many problems, not least was that as the cable-laying steamer *Fusilier* approached Scilly it came to the end of its cable! With an excited reception committee waiting on the shores of St Mary's, and anxious company officials insisting that time was running out, the desperate cable engineer made a bold decision. He ordered the ship to steam 'full ahead', snapping the cable. The ship entered the shallows of Penninis Head towing a few hundred yards of cable, to the cheers of the crowd and the approval of the Government Inspector who was convinced that Cornwall and the Isles of Scilly were now linked. A touch of mild electrical trickery indicated that signals were being received, and the cable was declared to be 'successfully laid'. The company got their compensation, and after a little 'checking and consolidation', the Isles of Scilly got their cable.

South West Peninsula Coastal Path

Without wires on Pedn-mên-an-mere: On the headland of Pedn-mên-an-mere stands a curious relic of a strange event in the history of communications.

In 1901 the scientist Marconi erected transmitter masts on Poldhu Cliffs, 17 miles *26·5 km* to the east, across Mounts Bay (see page 45). From there he succeeded in transmitting a message across the Atlantic by the great wonder of wireless.

News of this event caused some concern to the companies providing links all over the world by cable, not least to the Eastern Telegraph Company establishment at Porthcurno. It seemed sensible to them to erect a similar mast, hoping in some way to intercept these strange signals, and to find out what was going on. This they did on this headland. Whether they learned anything or not, the story doesn't reveal. The mast stood until a suspicious War Department ordered its destruction in 1914 'for security reasons'. All that remains of the venture is the rusting cage; the base of the fallen mast.

Radio is now a familiar feature in the bizarre world of industrial espionage. Perhaps here on Pedn-mên-an-mere is where it all began!

A cruel coast: This Footpath-Touring route follows a coastline which is beautiful and spectacular. With the mildest climate of the whole British Isles, its tropical plants, its pools of clear blue, and its green sea, it is popularly known as the Cornish Riviera.

However, the mariner knows another side. This most southerly stretch of Britain's coast, the 'gatepost' of the English Channel, lies in the path of some of the worst weather in the world. Wild south-westerly gales, and quickly developing sea mists, test both vessels and men. And this coast, so impressive for the land walker, presents a forbidding system of hazards, with hidden reefs, rocky headlands, and sinister lowlands. Hundreds of ships, and thousands of men have died here.

On the first day of this Footpath-Touring adventure we saw the twin peaks of the Brisons, $\frac{3}{4}$ mile *1·25 km* out from Cape Cornwall (see page 13).

This treacherous group has ripped the bottom out of many unsuspecting vessels. In 1842, the *St Austell*, bound from Newport to Penzance with a cargo of coal foundered here. A year later the *Whisper* met the same fate. Ten years later these same rocks claimed the brig *George*. But the worst was probably the wreck of the 250-ton brig *New Commercial* which piled on to them in dense fog on 11 January 1851. Furious seas began immediately to break up the ship and the crew of nine, and the Ship's Master and his wife, scrambled out to cling to the rocks. However a huge wave brushed them all into the sea and seven drowned. One, Isaac Williams, grabbed part of the rigging and paddled away to be rescued over near Sennen Cove. Captain Saunderson and his wife scrambled back on to the rocks and crouched there for two days and a night, the seas too rough for a rescue to be attempted. However, when the seas subsided a little, the Revenue cutter *Sylvia* got close enough to fire a rocket and line. The Captain tied the line about his wife's waist and bade her jump into the foaming sea. After some hesitation she took a leap, but as she did, three mighty waves dashed her back on to the rocks, threatening to take them both and what remained of the ship too. Mrs Saunderson was finally hauled ashore along with her husband but she died before reaching Sennen Cove.

A stone can still be found in Sennen Cove churchyard with the legend, 'To Mary, beloved wife of Captain Saunderson, who was shipwrecked on the Brisons and afterwards perished while being drawn through the waves. Aged 34 years.'

In hotels and pubs all round this coast you will see photographs and relics of similar disasters, losses, and brave rescues.

Today, with all the sophisticated navigational aids available, these rocks still take their toll. And the Coastguard service, the lifeboat crews, and the young men of the Royal Naval Helicopter Rescue Service, maintain a constant fight, and take great risks, to save the lives of those who go down to the sea in ships.

Cornwall's Fair Traders: It is not possible to walk this coastline without being very aware of the importance that smuggling once played in the life of Cornwall. Every creek, every cove, presents itself as a possible landing-place. Every steep cliff path suggests a route for struggling contraband-carriers. Every bend of the coast path becomes an ideal observation point for Revenue men.

It was Edward I, in 1275, who introduced excise duty on all wool, leather, and skins, exported from England to encourage home industries and raise finance.

However, customs duties were soon applied to imports, and smuggling became a way of getting round this hindrance of free trade. The West Country smugglers declared themselves to be England's 'free-traders'.

This corner of England became the centre of a great activity, illegally importing, in great quantities, tea, brandy, rum, tobacco, silks, and muslins. In 1783 a Parliamentary Report estimated that 300 English vessels were continuously involved in the trade. It was thought that from 1780 to 1783, 13 000 000 gallons of brandy, and 2 000 000 lb of tea had escaped customs duty. The officers of His Majesty's Excise and Customs fought a constant and sometimes dangerous battle against this tide.

In 1815, at the peak of the smuggling boom, no less than 1,425 types of goods were subject to duty, ranging from handkerchiefs to playing-cards. (The tax on playing-cards remained in force until 1960!)

Smuggling became a highly organised affair, with 'Venturers' supplying the capital and commissioning suitable vessels. 'Spotsmen' were responsible for ensuring that 'the coast was clear' of Revenue men. 'Batmen', armed with 'bats' and cudgels, acted as security guards. 'Tub-carriers' did the strenuous carrying of barrels and cases.

A vast legend has developed on smuggling methods and the ruses developed to defeat the Preventive men.

One device was 'crop-sowing'. This involved dropping overboard, at pre-arranged spots, barrels roped together and weighted, to be recovered under cover of darkness, when it was safe to do so. Long immersion often meant that spirits would become tainted with sea water, and in most pubs on this Footpath-Touring route, you can still buy Lovage and Shrub, both of which were used to disguise this in brandy and rum respectively.

False bottoms on boats, disguised cargoes, and sectioned barrels were all employed to hide contraband.

The tub-carriers employed various tricks. It was not unknown for ponies and donkeys to be shaved and greased to prevent them being grabbed by pursuing Revenue men. There are stories that horses were trained to obey special commands, and that a Revenue officer's 'Whoa!' would send the beast galloping away along the cliffs as fast as his load would permit.

But times have changed, and now smuggling is a thing of the past. (Incidentally, what exactly are those men doing down there on the beach?)

Footpath-Touring

Further information on Footpath-Touring with check-lists suggesting how to keep kit within weight limits and a wealth of other advice and useful tips are included in the publication *Footpa[illegible]ouring with Ken Ward. An Introduction, published by Jarrold o[illegible]ch.*

Other Footpath-Touring titles: *E[illegible]oo[illegible]Lorna Doone*
T[illegible]B[illegible]Lakeland

Emergency telephone numbers

Police stations: Penzance: Penalverne Drive 0736 62395.
Helston: Godolphin Road 03265 2414

Doctors: Pendeen: Dr Kiloh, next to Boscaswell Stores 0736 63361.
Penzance Hospital: West Cornwall Hospital, St Clare Street 0736 62382.
Mullion: The Health Centre, Nansmellyon Road 0326 240379/240212